SUSSEX
Murders

David Briffett

First published in 1990 by
Ensign Publications
2 Redcar Street
Southampton SO1 5LL

Publisher: David Graves
Edited by: Roy Gasson Associates
Typesetting by: PageMerger, Southampton

Printed and bound in the UK by Bell & Bain, Thornliebank, Glasgow.

British Library Cataloguing in Publication Data
Briffett, David
Sussex murders.
1. East Sussex. West Sussex, East & West Sussex. Murder, history
I. Title
364.1523094225

ISBN 1 85455 045 4

CONTENTS

1   THE ROMEO ROGUE   5
The Murder of Emily Kaye, 1924

2   THE CHICKEN-RUN SCANDAL   20
The Murder of Elsie Cameron, 1924

3   GRUESOME LEFT LUGGAGE   34
The Murder of Violet Kaye, 1934

4   THE BODY IN THE PARK   49
The Murder of Joan Woodhouse, 1948

5   FRIDAY THE THIRTEENTH   65
The Acid-bath Murders, 1944–49

6   THE DOCTOR AND THE ROLLS ROYCE   86
The Acquisitive Career of Dr Bodkin Adams

7   DEATH IN THE ARUN   106
The Killing of Jonathan Lewis, 1980

8   THE BODY IN THE BOOT   125
The Murder of James Sergeant, 1984

9   GET THE PRIME MINISTER!   140
The Brighton Bombing, 1984

INDEX   160

ACKNOWLEDGMENTS

I am specially indebted to members of Sussex Police force in the compilation of this book, both in making available important records and affording me many hours of their valuable time participating in interviews.

My personal thanks are due to The Chief Constable Roger Birch; the head of Sussex CID, Detective Chief Superintendent Roger Hills; Det. Supt. Bryan Grove, of Horsham; Det. Chief Supt. Gordon Harrison, of Brighton; Supt. Bernie Wells, of Horsham; and Neville Poulsom, administration support officer at Sussex Police HQ.

I am also very grateful to John Sampson, chief photographer of the West Sussex County Times, for his considerable help in providing photographic work; to Kevin Gordon for the loan of rare pictures and to Ann Williams for valuable research assistance.

SOURCES

Original documents: The Public Record Office, London; West Sussex County Record Office, Chichester; East Sussex County Record Office, Lewes; library reference sections at Brighton, Worthing and Horsham.

Newspapers: West Sussex County Times, Horsham; West Sussex Gazette, Arundel; Eastbourne Herald, Eastbourne; The Evening Argus, Brighton.

Books: *Bernard Spilsbury. His Life and Cases.* Douglas G. Browne and E.V. Tullett. (Harrap).

Who Framed Colin Wallace? Paul Foot. (Macmillan).

The Trial of Dr. Adams. Sybille Bedford. (Simon and Schuster).

Easing The Passing: The Trial of Dr. John Bodkin Adams. Patrick Devlin. (Bodley Head).

Two Men Were Acquited. Percy Hoskins. (Secker and Warburg).

Forty Years of Murder. Professor Keith Simpson. (Harrap).

The Acid Bath Murders. David Briffett. (Field Place Press).

In The Face of Fear. Harvey Thomas. (Marshalls).

1

THE ROMEO ROGUE

The Murder of Emily Kaye, 1924

Patrick Herbert Mahon, perhaps the most wicked criminal ever to walk on Sussex soil, was a charmer. With his square jaw, curly black hair, intriguing dark eyes and a good selection of smart suits, plus the slick tongue of an Irishman, he seemed always able to attract desirable women into his company and his bed. And, always, he seemed able to extricate himself, without difficulty, from these affairs.

That was until he met Emily Beilby Kaye. He swept her off her feet, snatching her away from the boredom of her office typewriter into a passionate affair. But when the time came to escape, this time he was trapped. And only desperate measures seemed to offer him escape.

Born in Liverpool in 1890, the son of a middle-class Irish immigrant family, Mahon began as a good Catholic and was even for a time a Sunday-school teacher. But in his twenties he began to haunt the racecourses and gamble heavily and he became involved in a series of frauds and thefts.

When he was just 21, he married a pretty 18-year-old named Mavourneen whom he had first met at school. It was a runaway marriage, involving a secret ceremony held after the bride's parents opposed the wedding because of her youth. Within a year, though, Mahon disappeared from both his home and his workplace after swindling his employer out of £123 in forged cheques. The

Emily Kaye *(Photo: Eastbourne Gazette)*   Patrick Mahon *(Photo: Eastbourne Gazette)*

police found him spending his gains on another woman in the Isle of Man. As a first offender, the magistrates bound him over, but when he later made off with £60 from a Wiltshire dairy firm a judge at Dorchester Assizes sent him to prison for a year.

For a while he tried to make a go of marriage again with the forgiving Mavourneen. They lived together in the Wiltshire town of Calne and had two children, a son and a daughter. He worked as a bookie's clerk at the local racecourse and for some time managed to escape the attentions of the law.

Then, in 1916, it all went wrong. Looking for easy cash, Mahon tried to rob the Sunningdale branch of the National Provident Bank. He broke in during the night but was disturbed by a woman servant who was sleeping on the premises. He promptly attacked her with a hammer that he carried, inflicting some nasty head injuries.

Most thwarted burglars would have run for it, but Mahon, realizing that the woman might identify him, proceeded to make amorous advances to her. While kissing and fondling the dazed woman he explained that he had not meant to harm her and asked her forgiveness. But he had over-estimated his charms. He was taken before Mr Justice Darling at Guildford Assizes and sentenced to five years' imprisonment.

For Mavourneen, left to look after the children while her husband was behind bars, times must have been almost unbearably hard and, when her baby son died, almost unbearably sad. She survived, though, managing to hold down a responsible job with Consols Automatic Aerators at Sunbury on Thames, in the London suburbs. Her love for her jailbird husband remained constant throughout. She kept his criminal record secret and, when he was released, she placed her hard-won integrity at stake by persuading her boss to give Mahon a job as a travelling salesman.

The role of a salesman on the move seemed to suit Mahon well, and the couple resumed family life in a home at Pagoda Avenue, Richmond. Mahon became honorary secretary to a bowls club. Family, social and working life all seemed to be going well. Even when, in 1923, Consols fell into financial difficulty and Mahon must have feared for his job, it turned out to be to his advantage. A firm of chartered accountants based at Copthall Avenue, Bloomsbury, took over as receivers and managers and promoted him to sales manager at the very considerable salary of £750 a year.

In his new job, Mahon often had to report to the firm's offices in Bloomsbury. And there he met – and fell for – an attractive shorthand-typist, Emily Kaye. Tall, fair-haired Emily, at 37 still, surprisingly, unattached, was in many ways an unlikely target for Mahon's roving eyes. She was far from the office flirt – a cousin of hers who lived in Hailsham in Sussex said of her: "I never heard her use a slang word, and she was clean from head to toe. A better girl never walked the earth."

There is no doubt, though, that she warmly welcomed Mahon's attentions. She may, too, have felt that he presented her last chance of married happiness and certainly she could not have wished to continue living indefinitely at the Green Cross Club, residential hostel for girls in Guildford Street, Bloomsbury, that was her home and where Mahon became a frequent visitor.

By early 1924 Emily was almost certainly looking towards a permanent relationship with Mahon. What was going on inside Mahon's mind it is impossible to tell. He had not left his wife and he may have felt trapped in his relationship with Emily. He would by now have found it difficult to disentangle himself from her. She was pregnant by him and she knew at least a little about his unsavoury past – by a remarkable chance, while she was clearing out a drawer, she had stumbled on a 1916 newspaper cutting that reported in graphic detail Mahon's jailing for the foiled bank raid. Clearly, his respectable, well-paid job would be at risk if Emily revealed what she knew to his employers.

Given her pregnancy, her dangerous knowledge and her determination and strong-mindedness it must have seemed to Mahon that this was an affair that he could not end as easily as he had some others in the past – and it was an affair that was becoming too intense for his comfort.

There was no doubt in Emily's mind that they were heading for a long-term future together. In March 1924 she was displaying a diamond and sapphire engagement ring and she wrote to her sister saying that she and "Pat" were planning a new life in South Africa. Then she left her job and withdrew her £600 savings, giving £300 to Mahon and changing much of the remainder into foreign currency. On April 7 she gave up her room at the Green Cross Club and moved out. She wrote to one of her friends, a Miss Warren, saying that she and Pat were "together" and that they would be going to Paris for the Easter weekend, would have a short stop-over in London and then depart for their "final journey".

That letter was the last that anyone ever heard from her. Mahon had totally deceived her. So, far from intending to marry her, he was planning to kill her.

He exchanged the three £100 notes given to him by Emily, using false names during each transaction. Then on April 4, he used the false name of Mr Waller when telephoning a Mr Muir in Victoria about a bungalow to let on the coast near Eastbourne. After viewing it, he agreed to take it for two months at a rent of 3½ guineas a week.

Ready to start a new life with the man she loved, Emily travelled to Eastbourne on April 7. She stayed at first in a small hotel, but after four days she moved into the bungalow Mahon had rented. Known as the Officer's House, Langney Cottages, this was a former coastguard station attractively sited on the edge of a shingle beach called the Crumbles on sweeping Pevensey Bay. The white-washed building had two spacious sitting rooms, two bedrooms, a kitchen and a scullery and was encircled by a brick and concrete wall.

In some situations it might have been called romantic. But it was also isolated. And Mahon was doing some rather unusual things for a man in the middle of an exciting love affair.

While in Richmond on the evening of Thursday April 10 – he was still going home to his wife on most days of the week – he chanced to meet a woman walking home in the rain. Ethel Duncan, who had been unhappily contemplating her lack of a job, was immensely cheered up by the attentions of this good-looking man. He arranged to take her out to dinner on the following Wednesday.

Next day, April 11, he helped Emily to move her large travelling trunk into their love nest, then returned to London, supposedly to begin making arrangements to secure a passport. On Saturday, April 12, he was in an ironmonger's shop in Victoria buying a large cook's knife and a tenon saw. Then he went back to the bungalow and Emily and he spent three nights together.

Emily met an appalling death on Tuesday, April 15. Precisely how she was killed will never be known – so little was left of her body that even Britain's finest pathologist, Sir Bernard Spilsbury, could not come to a definitive judgement. Most probably, Mahon attacked her suddenly from behind while she was standing in the sitting room, swinging a massively violent blow to the back of her head with an axe that had been used for breaking coal. He may then have finished her off by strangling her as she lay on the floor.

It may well be that Mahon was afterwards in a state of shock, for all he was able to do immediately was to drag the body to the spare bedroom, cover it up and lock the door. But his mind was still clear enough to recall his dinner date next day with Ethel Duncan; he sent her a telegram suggesting that they meet at Charing Cross Station.

That Wednesday he met Ethel as arranged and coolly entertained her to dinner. During the evening he invited her to spend the coming Easter weekend with him at the bungalow, and she, in her loneliness, agreed. The risk he took in inviting another woman to the bungalow where Emily's murdered body still lay beggars calculation.

On the morning of Good Friday, back at the bungalow, Mahon began disposing of Emily's body. He had decided to dismember it and to get rid of the pieces over the few weeks remaining on his lease of the bungalow.

Moving the body into a small bath in the scullery, he put the saw and knife he had bought in Victoria to work. He cut off pieces of convenient size and parcelled them up, some in clothing and some in brown paper tied with string. He put the parcels in Emily's trunk in the spare bedroom and sprinkled disinfectant powder over them. Smaller items he placed in a biscuit tin and two large stewpans from the kitchen. The removal of the head gave even the cold-blooded Mahon pause. He admitted that he thought for a long time before touching it, but eventually he severed it from the body with the saw and placed it inside the trunk.

That same evening he went to meet Ethel Duncan at Eastbourne railway station. Together they spent the rest of Easter weekend in the bungalow. Not once did Ethel have reason to suspect that Mahon had anything to hide. She did get a quick look into the spare bedroom and saw a large trunk there, but shortly afterwards Mahon screwed up the door, explaining that he had promised to secure it because he was "looking after a lot of valuable books for a friend". She did notice a bandage around Mahon's wrist, but he explained that away by saying that he had hurt himself saving a woman falling from a bus. She did see a lady's hairbrush, a pair of shoes and some cosmetics, but Mahon, who had talked about his "disastrous marriage", said that they belonged to his wife, who had been down on the previous weekend. She saw the sitting room, the scene of murder four days previously, but there was nothing to arouse her suspicions. Her host was perfectly at ease throughout and he had obviously done a very thorough job of cleaning up after the killing.

On Easter Monday, Ethel returned to her London home, leaving Mahon with the problem of disposing of Emily's remains. Tuesday morning he built a large fire in the sitting-room grate. The severed head had been much on his mind for several days and he wanted it out of the way. Soon it was burning fiercely on its home-made funeral pyre. Mahon later told his lawyer that the day he burned the head had been a stormy one and that, as Emily's long, fair hair flamed up, her dead eyes suddenly opened and at the same moment there was a clap of thunder. Petrified, he had fled from the house. Whether or not he was dramatizing we cannot know – he was, after all, a practised and convincing liar. In either case, eventually the fire did its job and Mahon crushed the bone fragments into dust with a poker.

The head disposed of, he used the bungalow's two grates to burn other parts of the body, including the legs, and portions of the arms. Emily had been three months pregnant, so he must also have somehow got rid of the uterus and its contents. Three days later he was left with just the torso.

Perhaps because he thought the bungalow's chimneys had been producing too much smoke or perhaps because he found the torso too unwieldy to burn, he now decided on a new method of disposal. He began hacking portions from the torso, boiling them in stewpans in the kitchen, and then cutting them into smaller pieces. These he wrapped in bits of Emily's clothing and placed inside a Gladstone travelling bag. While journeying by train to Waterloo, he simply threw them, unwrapped, out of the carriage window at various points along the track.

Given a little more time, he might have got away with it. Perhaps, in another week or so, all the remains of Emily Kaye would have been reduced to cinders, or distributed around the fringes of the southern rail network, no doubt to be devoured by scavenging animals. But he was not to be given that time.

The Officers House on Crumbles beach, Pevensey Bay, Langley. A photograph taken by Det. Insp. William McBride, New Scotland Yard, May 3, 1924.

Back at the marital home in Richmond, his wife Mavourneen had at last begun to be suspicious. Right up to the murder weekend of April 11-12, Mahon had been returning most evenings to Mavourneen and their child as though coming home from work. But when he stayed away first over that weekend and then over the Easter weekend she had become concerned. Telegrams she received from him, sent from Eastbourne, Bexhill and Vauxhall Bridge Road, with lame excuses about his whereabouts, failed to comfort her.

She may have feared that he was seeing another woman, but her chief worry was that he might be haunting the racecourses and involved in gambling again. So, when he was away once more, over the weekend of April 25-26, she began a systematic search through the pockets of his many suits, hoping for some information.

What she found was a cloakroom ticket for the left-luggage office at Waterloo Station. This was not in itself alarming, or even enlightening, but Mavourneen thought it might be a clue to what was going on – and if her husband had returned to the world of betting that was something she was determined to stop. So she said nothing of her discovery to Mahon when he returned home that week, but instead enlisted the help of a private investigator, John Beard, a former detective inspector with the railway police.

Four days later, on Thursday, May 1, she and Beard went to Waterloo, presented the ticket and received in exchange a Gladstone bag. It was locked, but Beard, probing one end, found something that sent him straight into a phone box to make a call to Scotland Yard.

As a result of that phone call, Detective Chief Inspector Percy Savage set a trap. Mavourneen, still not knowing the contents of the bag, was sent home to put the ticket back into the pocket where she had found it. The bag was replaced in the left-luggage office, after the police had taken from inside a small sample of cloth which revealed human blood. Two detective constables, Frew and Thompson, were left to keep watch on the office.

Mavourneen spent that Thursday night at home with her husband. It was to be their last night together.

True to his routine, on Friday, May 2, Mahon set out to spend a fourth weekend at Eastbourne ridding himself of the now rotting evidence. Dressed in a smart dark brown lounge suit, brown tie, brown shoes, with a soft brown hat on his head and a folded umbrella in his leather-gloved hands, he strode up to the Waterloo office to retrieve the Gladstone bag at 6.15 p.m.

Within moments of it being in his hand, two policemen were at his side. Protesting loudly, he was taken to Cannon Row police station. There Savage confronted him with the bag's contents: a torn pair of silk bloomers, two pieces of white silk, a blue silk scarf, each stained with blood and grease, one large cook's knife, some disinfectant powder and a canvas tennis-racket bag with the initials E.B.K. marked on it.

Asked to explain the blood, Mahon replied: "I am fond of dogs, and I suppose I have carried home meat for the dogs in it". Told that it was human blood, he repeated: "Dog's meat, dog's meat".

The interrogation went on into the early hours of Saturday morning. Then, finally, Mahon admitted to knowledge of the death of Emily Kaye and the disposal of her remains. "I suppose you know everything. I will tell you the truth," he told Savage.

His version of the truth was that Emily had met her death by accident. And by then there was so little left of her body that the police scientists were going to have quite a challenge in order to prove him a liar.

A few hours later, Savage and another officer, Inspector Hall, entered the Officer's House. The stench that permeated the rooms was so foul that they had to fling open the shuttered windows to let in the outside air. No effort had been made to hide anything. The police surgeon who was called in found the charred remains of bones in two fireplaces, two large stewpots containing boiled flesh, a biscuit tin holding some intestines and the heart and a square leather hat-box holding thirty pieces of boiled flesh.

Inside a large fibre travelling trunk with the initials E.B.K. on both sides were four grisly parcels wrapped in pieces of clothing and paper. These the surgeon unwrapped. One contained a mass of decaying flesh and sawn-up bone. A third held part of the chest and backbone. The fourth contained the left side of the chest with its ribs hacked away from the backbone, plus the upper end of an arm bone.

Evidence of the carnage was everywhere. More bone fragments were found in an ash can in the scullery, a galvanized-iron bath was smeared with grease and blood, lying on a carpet was a bloodstained tenon saw and in the scullery was an axe, its handle broken and its head stained with blood.

The Home Office pathologist, Bernard Spilsbury, who had been at the centre of numerous sensational Scotland Yard inquiries, described the scene at the Officer's House as the most gruesome he had ever come across in his long career.

During a spring Sunday, Spilsbury made a detailed eight hour survey of Mahon's handiwork as crowds of horrified onlookers began to gather around the walls of the bungalow. Some of them would have seen the pathologist clad in his white apron and rubber gloves working for three hours at a small table in the garden surrounded by a team of grimly silent detectives.

The public clamour continued on the following Tuesday when Mahon was charged with murder at Hailsham Court. He told the magistrates, simply: "I have already made a statement. It was not murder as my statement clearly shows". Eastbourne solicitor Mr C.W. Mayo then asked permission for Mahon to attend the inquest.

This led to what must be one of the most bizarre of all inquests. It was opened next day in the sitting room of the bungalow. Mahon was led in under tight police escort. About a thousand sightseers surrounded the building and he could hear their boos and jeers as he went in and out, but saw nothing, covering his head with a heavy overcoat.

While Mahon was on remand in custody, the police made a determined search for parts of Emily's body so that the cause of her death could be established. In particular, teams of officers were ordered to find the head. Mahon had said that he had burned it, but there was no reason to believe him. And Spilsbury, in spite of his exhaustive work at the bungalow, could not find a single fragment that linked to the head or neck. It had vanished apparently without trace. Sniffer dogs were brought in to comb the beach, tons of shingle were raked, refuse tips were scoured, the garden was dug up and the railway tracks were walked. There was much excitement when some bone fragments and teeth were recovered from a tip at Langney, but these turned out not to be human.

Doubtful that a human head could be completely destroyed by burning on an ordinary fire, Spilsbury experimented using a sheep's head and found to his surprise that it was reduced to ashes in four hours. It looked as though Mahon had done exactly what he said he had done.

Despite this gap in the evidence, it was a confident Mr Sefton Cohen who opened the case for the prosecution before the Hailsham magistrates late in May. There was never any doubt that Mahon would be sent for trial. The resumed inquest, which was held shortly afterwards, was even more damning. After the jury had listened to an enormous amount of detailed evidence, the like of which would never be presented at a modern-day coroner's inquiry, the foreman rose to declare: "On the evidence you have placed before us, we have come to the conclusion that the deceased was Emily Beilby Kaye; we find that she was murdered; and we find that she was murdered by Patrick Herbert Mahon".

With Sir Henry Curtis Bennett leading for the prosecution, the trial opened at Lewes Assizes some six weeks later, on July 15.

Ethel Duncan, tall, heavily veiled, a handkerchief held to her face, was in considerable distress; she sobbed as she took the oath. When the judge, Mr Justice Avory, asked her if she recognized the prisoner she astonished everyone by replying, "No, I have not". She cried out, "Please, no!" when the judge ordered Mahon to stand up in the dock, then burst into tears and through her sobs finally confirmed, "I recognize him".

Ethel struggled through a gruelling hour in the witness box. There was surprise in court when she said that she had seen nothing unusual during the Easter weekend she had spent at the bungalow. She had noticed that the coal scuttle had been slightly damaged, and that Patrick had four bruises at the top of his arm, but there had been nothing to arouse her suspicion.

During the second day of the trial, one of the jurymen, overwhelmed by the horror of the evidence, turned pale and collapsed. After a short adjournment he fainted again and was said to be too unwell to continue. Then a second juryman pleaded illness. Two replacement jurymen had to be sworn in and all the evidence had to be repeated for their benefit.

Mahon sustained a daunting five hours and forty minutes giving his evidence. Wearing a brand-new suit, he was immaculate from head to toe. Now, just as he had so often successfully captivated women, he set out to charm a jury. And he put on quite a performance. He did, though, lose control for a moment during the third day. He was being questioned by his own counsel, Mr J. D. Cassels, about the disposal of the head. A summer storm was raging outside and suddenly the courtroom shook from the noise of a thunderclap. Mahon lost his confident air, turned white and gripped the edge of the witness box convulsively.

Mahon stuck steadfastly to his story that Emily's death had been accidental. Together with his defence team he began to portray Emily in a totally new light. He said that he had met her through his work, that she became very fond of him, and that several months after their first meeting they became lovers. He discovered, to his surprise, that she was "a woman of the world" and certainly no innocent.

Just before Christmas, 1923, she had lost her job and wanted to see him more often, but he was unwilling to get too deeply involved. Feeling "sorry for her" he continued their meetings and when Emily begged him to give up everything and go abroad with her he firmly declined the invitation – though, for the purpose of "gaining time", he agreed to think it over. Emily then pressed him to go away with her for a holiday so that she could convince him of her love. But, again he refused to entertain the notion. Only later, when he learned that she had given up her room at the Green Cross Club, did he rent the bungalow at Eastbourne.

This was not quite how Emily herself related her position in letters to relatives. Mahon was doing his best to conjure up a vision of a man being reluctantly drawn into a relationship he did not seek.

He told the court that when he visited Emily at the bungalow on Saturday, April 12, she told him that she was charmed by it. At one point she said to him, "Pat, old boy, you will never regret it, and I will make it up to you for all you have lost".

However, she became upset when she realized he would not be staying permanently and another argument began when they travelled to London together on the following Tuesday with the intention of Mahon going to the passport office. When Emily discovered that he had not been there, she became "furious".

But she had cooled down by the time they returned to Eastbourne later in the day. During the evening, Emily sat writing letters while Mahon brought the coal scuttle in and lit the fire, breaking up large bits of coal with an axe. They began to talk about their future. Mahon's version of the conversation went like this:

"Pat", Emily said, "I am determined to settle this matter one way or another tonight. These letters and my other actions mean that I have burned my boats and for me there is no turning back. Can't you realize Pat how much I love you? You are everything to me and I can never share you with another. Do write to Richmond and finish up there."

"I can't do that. Why can't we be pals?"

"What's the use of palship to me, to one of my nature?"

"That's all I can offer. I can't give up all that I hold dear. I would rather tell my wife the whole thing."

According to Mahon, Emily finally snapped at this point. She became "angry, hysterical and distraught". As he moved to leave the room, she caught hold of the axe, which was lying on the table, and threw it straight at him, catching him a blow on the shoulder. The axe then glanced off him to hit the framework of the door.

"I was astounded by the attack. In a second Miss Kaye leaped across the room, clutching at my face", he told the court. Then, suddenly, he broke down in tears, doubling his body up across the witness box. Still sobbing, he continued the story:

"I did my best to keep her off and we struggled backwards and forwards. I realized I was dealing with a woman who was almost mad. She began to get the better of me. I pushed her from me and we both fell over an easy-chair towards the fireplace. Miss Kaye's head hit the cauldron. I think I must have fainted with fear and shock. When I became conscious of what was happening, Miss Kaye was lying near the coal scuttle and blood was flowing from her head on to the floor. She was motionless. I tried to rouse her and I think I must have fainted again. The next thing I remember is getting up and dashing water into her face and calling her by name. I must have gone half-mad. I then went out into the garden and went crazy with fright and fear.

"Hours later", Mahon said, towards daybreak he returned to the bungalow. He suddenly realized he had been a fool not to call for assistance and the knowledge that Emily was dead "got into my brain". Eventually he decided that the only course was to conceal everything.

"Did you desire the death of Miss Kaye?" asked Mr Cassels. Now quite calm again, Mahon replied: "Never at any time".

Mahon's performance had been masterly. Now his defence counsel did a fine job for him. In his final plea to the jury, Cassels urged them to ignore the immorality, to forget the ghastly details, but simply to concentrate on how Emily Kaye had died. That she was normally of "a quiet disposition" he admitted, but "Heaven knows no rage like love to hatred turned, Nor hell no fury like a woman scorned". And was the well-dressed, softly spoken gentleman in the dock really an "inhuman monster"; was he not rather "the victim of an extra-ordinary combination of circumstances"?

The jury had a straightforward choice. Perhaps they were tempted to believe in the slick-tongued Irishman in the dock before them. They had, of course, no knowledge of his previous record and they could have seen him as an unfortunate swept along in a tragic sequence of events that had somehow got out of control.

But there were just too many awkward things to explain away.

There was the kitchen knife and the saw. In Mahon's first statements to the police he said that he had bought them on April 17, two days after Emily's death. But a duplicate invoice from the ironmonger, produced in the magistrates court, showed that they had been sold on April 12 – the Saturday before the death.

Then there was the cause of death. Mahon said it was a fall on to the coal scuttle. But the pathologist Bernard Spilsbury had given it as his expert opinion both at the inquest and at the trial that such a fall "would not have been capable of inflicting such injuries to the head as to cause rapidly fatal results." The scuttle was flimsily made and more likely than not would have simply crumpled up under a heavy blow. Had Emily fallen on to it she would not have received injuries severe enough to kill her instantly – there would have been time to call for medical help.

Finally, there was Ethel Duncan. If anything destroyed Mahon's character in front of the jury it was his assignation with this woman while he had a wife and child at home in Richmond and a pregnant mistress in a bungalow at Eastbourne. It had been a casual pick-up en route between the coast and home. He had sent Ethel a telegram on Tuesday, April 15 – the day that Emily died – inviting her out to lunch on the Wednesday, an appointment he had kept. Together they had spent the whole of the Easter weekend enjoying each other's company inside the bungalow of horrors. Mahon explained this extraordinary event in court by saying that he "needed human companionship". And here, surely, he must have forfeited the sympathy, and the understanding of the jury.

Even before the verdict of guilty came in, the bungalow on the Crumbles was

The locked bedroom containing the trunk in which Mahon kept the body of Emily Kaye.

being turned into a macabre shrine. An enterprising group of people had taken over the lease and were charging a shilling a head for guided tours. Visitors had the chance to handle some of the exhibits, among which were stewpans and a poker that the police had already returned. The guides made much out of Mahon's lifestyle, producing his bottles of hair cream and scent in the bedroom, and spoke sympathetically of the innocent Emily. As the queues built up, they arranged for drinks to be served at the front gate. In the extraordinary summer of 1924, the Officer's House became one of the top seaside attractions in Sussex.

Not everyone favoured this morbid display and there were threats to burn down the bungalow. For two weeks it was closed to let tempers cool, but it re-opened after a facelift with a new entry fee of 1s. 2d. Now visitors came by coachloads to share in the atmosphere of a major event. On the day Mahon was executed, Wednesday, September 3, the guides delayed allowing the first visitors in until two minutes after nine as their own peculiar mark of respect.

The saddest of all the figures in this case was Mahon's wife, Mavourneen. She remained loyal to him to the end. From the death cell Mahon wrote her a final letter.

All my thanks for your letter received yesterday. I do quite understand dearest why you didn't manage to visit me this week. I did know of course – intuition if you like – how poorly you were and are.

In a sense, that is the hardest part of all this terrible trouble. For myself I would not mind so much if only I could help you. I can imagine, knowing how ill you were, what an ordeal you have had, and what may still have to follow. For remember darling that I have never doubted your faith. I have such a lot to be regretful about, not so much for myself, but about you and home. But you know where my love is.

All the wasted efforts, and the disappointed hopes – they constitute a big enough burden of sorrow, but the other hurts the most. Try and find some comfort in that knowledge, dear. Besides, darling, if there is a fearless human justice, my appeal will succeed and then there perhaps Divine providence will help.

For yourself, darling, all my love and worship. Pat.

2
THE CHICKEN-RUN SCANDAL
The Murder of Elsie Cameron, 1924

John Norman Holmes Thorne was born in Portsmouth in 1901. His mother died when he was only seven years old and his father, a naval boffin, remarried about a year later. The family moved to London in 1911, when Mr Thorne was promoted to engineering inspector and took up a post at the Admiralty. Norman seemed set to follow in his father's footsteps when, at the age of 14, he was apprenticed to an aero- and marine-engineering company. His apprenticeship completed, he saw war service with the Royal Navy Air Service.

There was nothing in these mundane beginnings to suggest that he would end his life on the gallows. Indeed he seemed to be following a highly moral way of life. From the age of 15 he was a Sunday School teacher and a Band of Hope speaker, at 16 he formed a natural history club and at 17 he founded and ran a troop of 160 boy scouts. After his demobilization he pursued his interest in chapel affairs ("I dislike high religion", he once wrote), taking a leading part in the Wesley Guild, which involved temperance and social work and organizing concerts and open-air gatherings of the faithful.

The unlikely agent of future tragedy was Elsie Cameron, a woman he had known since childhood – her family, like his, had lived in the London suburb of Kensal Rise. Now, in 1921, she was 22 and an active member of the same Wesleyan church as Norman. They were attracted to one another and, towards

Norman Thorne. The photograph was taken before he was charged in January, 1925. *(Photo: Press Association)*

the end of 1922, became engaged, with the approval of their parents. Elsie seems to have been an ordinary enough young woman – 5ft 3in tall and not particularly pretty – but she was rather emotional, perhaps even neurotic. But then Norman was not handsome – he had a big nose, protruding ears and baggy eyes. But he had grown into a solid young man with a strong, round face, bushy eyebrows and a smart head of hair.

After the war, Norman had obtained what appeared to be a very sound job in the experimental and electrical department of Fiat Motors in London. But a trade slump closed the works and threw him into a long period of unemployment. With the prospect of marriage before him he now made a bold bid to carve out a living for himself on the land. With a sum of £100 borrowed from his father, he purchased a field in the centre of rolling East Sussex countryside in Luxford Lane at Blackness close to the small town of Crowborough, and there he set up the fittingly named Wesley Poultry Farm.

He moved to the farm to live alone in a comfortless wooden building measuring just 7ft x 12ft, set amid the chicken huts and built originally to provide a brooding house. It contained only a primitive wood-burning stove, a writing desk, a narrow bunk bed, a table and a chair, while an oil lamp strung from the ceiling provided light. Norman made some effort to brighten the place up with pictures on the walls, but there was no cupboard space for keeping clothes and a washing line strung between two walls did not enhance the scene.

For two years, in often muddy conditions, he struggled to make a living from the hens. Elsie came down to visit at weekends, in between attempting to conquer periods of ill health and holding down a London typing job. Such were the conditions at the farm hut that she would simply spend the days there with Norman and his poultry, lodging at night with nearby families – at first Agnes and Edwin Piper of Pasture Villas and later Florence and Robert Cosham at Corona in Luxford Lane.

The prosperity that would have made marriage possible did not come, but the engagement endured. The young couple were together at the farm for the Christmases of 1922 and 1923 and in the summer between Elsie stayed for a six-week spell during which she managed to find temporary employment as a nursemaid in Crowborough.

Early in 1924, though, Norman formed a new friendship – with the altogether prettier and livelier Elizabeth Ann Coldicott, a dressmaker who lived with her mother at Springfield in South View Road, Crowborough. They first met at a Whitsuntide dance at Waterloo Hall and continued to meet at later dances, despite the continuing weekend visits by Elsie. At first the association was entirely open. Norman not only told 'Bessie' that he was engaged but introduced her to 'his intended' during one of her weekend visits.

But the relationship with the local girl blossomed quite quickly into a love affair. In September Bessie first agreed to visit the farm shed alone, "for tea". During November she called several times a week, staying for about two hours each evening.

"He told me he was engaged to Miss Cameron", she later confided to the police. "He said he would like to give her up only her nerves were so bad. He thought he would be marrying into trouble. He suggested that we should marry if he could break off the engagement. While in the hut we were just making love, I sat in one armchair on his knee."

Elsie sensed that she was losing Norman. Agnes Piper said that Elsie was, that autumn, "in a very nervous state," strained and suffering fits of depression. Florence Cosham noted the new relationship and thought that Norman and Bessie were planning to be together at Christmas 1924 and that Elsie would definitely not be welcome.

Good Christian that he was, Norman did make a genuine effort to be honest about the matter and admitted to Elsie during an exchange of letters that he found himself "between two fires" – having to choose between the childhood sweetheart to whom he was promised and the exciting new woman in his life. But he did not have the heart, or the courage, to tell Elsie that it was all over between them, that the engagement was off.

In that November the now desperate Elsie played her trump card: she wrote to tell Norman that she was pregnant, and that the baby was his. "You have absolutely broken my heart", she declared sadly. "I never thought you were capable of such deception. You are engaged to me and I have first claim on you. Well, Norman, I expect you to marry me, and finish with the other girl as soon as possible. My baby must have a name."

In a further bid to persuade him, she made an unexpected visit to Wesley Poultry Farm on Sunday, November 30, but was hustled back to Groombridge railway station and the London train in time for Norman and Bessie to meet that evening.

Five days later she tried again. This time, it seems, she was buoyed up by the prediction of a fortune teller, in whom she placed a naive trust, that she would marry in December. This time, too, she made a pathetic effort to make herself more attractive. It seems clear that her hopes were high that she could hold

Norman to their engagement and make him give up Bessie.

On the morning of Friday, December 5, Elsie – saying nothing of her plans to her father, commercial traveller Donald Cameron – went to the hairdressers. She emerged with a brand new hairstyle which was immediately noticed by her neighbour Bertha Motture. The two chatted for an hour. Elsie, who was wearing a ring containing rubies, proudly showed Bertha a new silk jumper and a pair of shoes. She was in a "very cheerful" mood. Then, at 2.00 p.m., with her belongings neatly packed in a small suitcase, she left Kensal Rise for Sussex.

That rail journey, a familiar part of her routine for more than two years, was to be the last of her life.

She arrived at the poultry farm late that afternoon, looking her very best, suitcase in hand, hoping for a loving reconciliation. She was met by a fiancée who had come to realize that he was not in love with her at all, that her claims on him were an intolerable oppression and that her pregnancy stood between him and his dreams of happiness with Bessie.

Her sudden, dramatic arrival on his doorstep, a court later decided, turned this decent, mild-mannered, chapel-going poultry farmer into a killer.

Precisely how Elsie met her death is a matter for conjecture. It seems certain that she died some time between 5.15 p.m., when she arrived at Welsey Poultry Farm, and 9.30 p.m., when Norman went to Crowborough station to meet Bessie and her mother returning from a trip to Brighton. She was probably clubbed with what the police later described as "a blunt instrument," maybe a wooden stake or possibly one of several Indian clubs kept in the hut. No bones were broken, but Elsie suffered serious bruising to her legs and arms; then two vicious blows to either side of her face which rapidly led to her death.

The circumstances have to be imagined because Norman Thorne never admitted to that attack.

It is certain, though, that after the death he behaved with remarkable coolness. As far as he was aware, no-one had seen Elsie arrive at his remote and lonely home, and he probably established from her that she had told no-one in London of her intended destination. If she vanished from sight now, no-one would ever know that she had set foot inside the hut.

With Elsie's battered body lying in or near the hut, Norman went off to meet his new love at the station. Coolly, he walked Bessie and her mother to their Crowborough home, and offered a goodnight kiss at her gate. Then he returned to the darkness of his chicken farm at about 11.30 p.m., there to spend a night of abject horror.

A police model of Thorne's bungalow used in court.

Working outside in the chill of a winter's night he used a strong hack-saw to carve the body into four sections. Then he must have spent most of the remaining hours of darkness digging.

He buried Elsie's suitcase and some of her belongings in a potato patch quite close to the farm gate. He put some of her valuables, including a gold wrist watch, into an Oxo tin, which he hid in the tool shed. He removed her outer woollen frock and other garments and burned them. The severed legs he tied together with string, wrapped in a parcel of sacking and buried nearly two feet deep in the clay of a chicken run. He dealt similarly with the torso and arms. He wrapped Elsie's severed head in sacking and crammed it into a tin box which he bound with string and buried close to the body, two feet down in the same chicken run.

Next afternoon he visited Bessie and later they spent a pleasant evening together at the cinema. Bessie noticed nothing at all out of the ordinary.

Elsie was, of course, missed but her father only began to be seriously concerned after five days passed without news of her. On December 10, assuming that her most likely destination would have been Crowborough, he sent off a telegram to Norman: "Elsie left Friday have heard no news has she arrived, reply". Thorne replied on the same day: "Not here open letters cannot understand".

Mr Cameron then went to the police and Elsie became an officially listed missing person. At first the search centred on London, where she had been last seen, but police in Sussex, led by Inspector George Edwards of Crowborough and Superintendent Isaac Budgen of Uckfield, also began enquiries. Thorne co-operated fully with them, allowing officers to check his land and to go through all the chicken huts and runs as well as his living accommodation; he even supplied a snapshot of Elsie for publication in the *Police Gazette*, while he was ready to offer his own helpful theories to any who would listen.

On December 13 he told Edwards that Mr Cameron was checking out a report that Elsie had been seen going to a house in Holloway. In a chat with Florence Cosham he suggested that Elsie might have committed suicide by jumping into the Thames, adding "what with the weather we have been having she might have been washed out to sea". In conversation with a local rose and fruit-grower, George Adams, he speculated that she had fallen exhausted somewhere and been taken away by gipsies, or "that the Mormons might have got hold of her". He told Elsie's sister that she had once threatened to throw herself out of a train.

His story to the police was that he had last seen Elsie on November 30. He had expected a further visit from her on Saturday, December 6. He had gone to Groombridge railway station on that day to collect her for a shopping trip in Tunbridge Wells, but she had not turned up and so he went alone, returning home at about 1.00 p.m.

Police enquiries took up much of December but failed to establish what had happened to Elsie. Two statements, though, from George Adams and from Albert Sands, who worked together at Jarvis Brook nurseries, interested the local police. Both men recalled having seen a young woman with a suitcase walking down Luxford Road at Blackness towards Thorne's farm some time after 5.00 p.m. on December 5. But when Superintendent Budgen put this to Thorne, he replied simply: "Yes, I've heard it got about, but I rather doubt it".

This was not evidence hard enough to cast any serious doubt on Thorne's version of events. He and Bessie spent that Christmas together and on January 1, 1925, he wrote her a long letter:

My Darling Bessie,

Looking back over the last few months I perceive many changes in my life. I don't think many fellows have had the ups and downs, and adventures in ten years of "life" as I have and now that I have contaminated your dear name with mine and gained your friendship and your love I think it only fair that you should know a little of my past … especially under the circumstances as they are at present …

I have been in love twice. The first just before I enlisted and this was dissolved soon after I came home (she isn't missing), the second was with Elsie which is more important. I have told you that I was fond of her and I want to be perfectly frank, dear, we were intimate but that was all, for no one will ever turn me against my principles.

I was never intimate with any other girl. Elsie had a strange disposition and strange parents, neither of which anyone seems to understand, particularly just now. They knew my love (which I now realise was really sympathy) was cooling after two years of her nervous state, and they tried to force her on to me.

However, my will was too strong for them and now they are showing their spite, as I understand Scotch people can by painting me as black as possible and doing me all the harm they can. I have only written this to let you see what's what.

What I want you to understand is that my love for you is honest and true, you are not the plaything of an hour to be thrown away when I leave Crowborough. Honour bright, darling I never felt for any girl as I do for you, it was easy to leave London to come to Crowborough, but it will be devilish hard to leave Crowborough for London. I have found the most wonderful thing in the world – love – pure and true.

Fate has often been unkind, but I believe meeting you is the richest blessing I have ever had and however some may talk and laugh at love, it is the sweetest and dearest thing I have found. I long to be able to lay my head on your loving breasts and know that you are mine. I shall strive to make you the happiest little girl in the world to show my thanks for your wonderful friendship during the terrible crisis we are passing through.

I cannot thank you enough dear heart, for no one knows the struggle that has raged within, but dearest of pals, you have pulled me through.

Love – Honour – Bessie. My watch words for '25.

Now and always, yours with all my love, Norman.

It is clear from this that Norman was becoming confident that the "terrible crisis we are passing through" was coming to end. The police enquiry had got nowhere and, by January 10 he must have thought that he had got clean away with it.

On that day his luck changed. Until then Mrs Annie Price of Blackness Cottages, although a near neighbour of Thorne's, had heard nothing about the missing Elsie – she did not often read newspapers and she did not listen to local gossip. But now, through a chance look at the local paper, she learned about the search for the missing woman and remembered what she had seen on December 5.

She had been on a half-hour walk to visit a friend at Jarvis Brook. On the way back, at about 5.15 p.m., when passing Wesley Poultry Farm, she spotted two men in the distance. One was Albert Sands, who "walks peculiar." Near them was a young woman carrying an attaché case. From only 15 yards away, Mrs Price watched her walk briskly through the farm gate and set off towards the first chicken shed.

Linked to the sightings of Adams and Sands recorded weeks earlier, this information assumed a great significance – so great that the Sussex Chief Constable decided to call on the immediate assistance of Scotland Yard, who responded by sending Chief Inspector John Gillan and Detective Sergeant Ambrose Askew to Sussex.

On the afternoon of January 14 there was a dramatic confrontation between the Yard men and Thorne at his farm hut, where they found him sitting in a chair holding a photograph of Bessie Coldicott.

"I have reason to believe that Elsie Cameron was seen alive on these premises at 5.15 p.m. on December 5 and I propose to search and take a statement," Gillan told him. Thorne replied: "I have heard rumours of her being here, but I do not believe them. You can search and I will render you every assistance and I am quite prepared to make a statement."

Later in the day the two Yard men did their best to unsettle Thorne during a long interview with him at Crowborough police station. But he stuck to his original version of events, telling them boldly: "I have nothing to fear". He offered no objection to the police digging on his land, provided only that they left his precious chicken runs alone!

A new search, this time by men from the Yard, of the chicken huts and Thorne's own hut, was no more successful than the first. But Gillan was not discouraged – many other possibilities were in his mind. Early next morning, on January 15, he set into motion a little agricultural exercise which involved P.C.

Trumpeters fanfare the Judge's arrival at Lewes Crown Court for the Thorne trial in 1925.

J.D. Cassels K.C. defence counsel for Norman Thorne.

John Philpott of the Sussex constabulary undertaking some random digging with a spade in the potato plot five yards from the gate. At precisely 8.25 a.m. the spade struck the buried suitcase, in which Elsie's easily identified clothes were still intact.

In that moment the game was up for Thorne and he must have known it at 9.30 a.m. when Gillan informed him: "You will now be detained and probably charged with causing the death of Elsie Cameron". Thorne made no reply and remained silent for the rest of the day, during which he was held in a police cell. Then, after obviously thinking matters through in great detail, at 8.10 p.m. he broke his silence with a request for a pencil and paper to make a new statement.

It was a simple story. Yes, Elsie had turned up on the Friday evening. She repeated that she was pregnant, that she intended to stay there for good, and wanted marriage. They had tea and talked together about the situation until at 9.30 p.m. he went out to meet Bessie. When he returned to the hut at 11.30 p.m. to his horror he found Elsie hanging from a roof beam on the end of his washing line. Fearing that, because of Bessie, he might be accused of causing Elsie's suicide, he had decided to get rid of the evidence. The dismembered body would be found under the ground in the first chicken pen inside the farm gate.

The detectives were not prepared to wait for daylight. A score of policemen, under Gillan and Askew from the Yard and Edwards from the Sussex constabulary, went to the poultry farm and, at 10.45 p.m. began digging by lamplight. There, just below the surface, they recovered two heavy parcels and one large tin box.

At the mortuary Gillan cut the string around the box and removed its lid to reveal the sacking-wrapped parcel inside. As he unrolled the sacking, out tumbled a female head, a significant bruise evident over the left eye. At 10.30 next morning they unwrapped the torso and legs. They found two dress rings on the left hand, and a birth mark on the upper arm.

Edwards found the Oxo tin with Elsie's valuables in the tool shed and P.C. Thomas Goodsell recovered a hacksaw from the hut. There was no doubt in the minds of the police. Thorne was charged with murder at 2.15 p.m on the same day.

Sir Bernard Spilsbury, the most experienced criminal pathologist of his generation, was called in to examine the remains. Perhaps surprisingly, he found no cuts or grazes to the body, and no broken bones. But he did identify eight significant bruises "all inflicted shortly before death and in the case of two of them they were immediately followed by death". He concluded: "The cause of death was shock due to the injuries on the face, head and limbs".

The remains of Elsie Cameron were buried in a sad little ceremony in Willesden on January 26.

The eminent King's Counsel appointed to defend Norman Thorne was Mr J.D. Cassels, the advocate who had defended Patrick Mahon. One month after Spilsbury's post-mortem, he arranged for exhumation of the body so that a pathologist appointed by the defence could make an independent examination. The task fell to Dr Robert Bronte, a flamboyant Irishman, former crown analyst to the Irish Government and in 1925 pathologist at Harrow Hospital in London.

When the trial began at Lewes Assizes on March 4, it soon became clear that a fierce battle would ensue over the medical evidence. On one side, for the defence, were ranged Bronte and seven other doctors whom Cassels had called upon; on the other, for the prosecution, was Spilsbury. The prosecution was outnumbered but the reputation of Spilsbury was truly formidable.

What could not be denied was the bruising to the body, though Bronte did his utmost to confuse the issue by arguing that some bruises were caused before death and some after. He also pointed out that there was no breaking of facial skin and no damage to the flimsy cheek-bones, both of which would have been expected if blows severe enough to kill had been inflicted.

Thorne's best hope of avoiding the gallows rested on his claim that Elsie had committed suicide and that his only offence was that he had concealed her body. Not once did he deviate from this story and Bronte caused the sensation of the trial when he revealed that in his medical examination of the body he found abnormal creases at the neck, which could have been made by a thin rope or cord. He had also found evidence of broken blood vessels at the neck, consistent with a hanging.

Spilsbury was, as always, quite dogmatic in his contrary opinion: "If the girl had hanged herself with a cord there would have been a groove in the neck, if there had been a washing cord as has been described. I found no indications of asphyxia whatever. In my examination I found no natural disease to account for death nor any indication external or internal that death had been caused by hanging."

What was a jury to make of such conflict?

They were assisted by some experiments carried out by the police. Gillan and Askew of the Yard had set out to test the strength of the 5ft 9in internal beam that supported the roof of Thorne's hut and from which he claimed Elsie had hanged herself. They had hung two half-hundredweight weights from a thick cord thrown over the beam and rested them on a chair standing 6ft 7½in below. When the chair was gently moved away and the weights allowed to hang for a

31

short time the string left a "decided dent" in the soft wood of the beam. In a second test they jerked the chair away so that the beam suddenly took the weight, as it might if a suicide had kicked away the chair. Although held only by three nails at each end, the beam bore the sudden weight, but this time the cord made an even deeper indentation in the wood. The implication, of course, was that, if Elsie had hanged herself from the beam, as Thorne claimed, the washing line would have left a mark on the wood. The beam was produced in court to show that it bore no such mark.

Nonetheless, Thorne's story, told so confidently from the witness box, coupled with Bronte's assertion that the medical evidence was consistent with suicide, was sufficient to cause doubt in many minds. But in the end the jury took just 25 minutes to find Thorne guilty of murder.

They may have been influenced by the knowledge that the police had found in Thorne's hut a collection of newspaper cuttings covering the trial of Patrick Mahon who, at a lonely Sussex bungalow only months before, had disposed of the body of a woman who had become an embarrassment to him, a woman who was pregnant and wanted to marry him. Did they think that Mahon's crime had inspired Thorne's?

A furious public debate ensued over the next four weeks; had there been a miscarriage of justice? The defence lawyers and others called for a reprieve. However, the Lord Chief Justice turned down pleas to appoint a medical commissioner to arbitrate on the conflicting medical evidence and the Home Secretary refused to intervene. Thorne was executed at Wandsworth on April 22, on what would have been Elsie's 27th birthday.

Long after the hanging, the case continued to occupy public attention. The schoolchildren of Sussex sang a sad little song about it: "Somewhere across the sea, there lies Elsie Cameron, Norman Thorne, he cut her up, he cut her up, so they say ....".

Even the final words of that innocent ditty, "so they say", contained a hint of the uncertainty that lingered in many minds. Then, and later, some quite important people questioned the verdict, including the author Sir Arthur Conan Doyle, the barrister Helena Normanton and writer/lawyer Edgar Lustgarten, whose work *Verdict in Dispute* was published more than 24 years later.

An uncomfortable feeling remained that a non-expert jury had been set the task of deciding between the opinions of two opposing pathologists, either of whom might have been right, with a man's life dependant on the outcome. It was suggested that Spilsbury's reputation was so unchallenged that his evidence

A rare and highly illegal view of British justice at work. The scene at Lewes Assizes as Norman Thorne gives his evidence.

was favoured over that of the less-well-known Bronte, even though Bronte had been supported by no fewer than seven other doctors – and it was possible that the great man might have made a mistake.

This huge discrepancy between the views of two knowledgeable men was disconcerting, but, after all, the case did not rely entirely on the medical evidence. The jury, after hearing and watching Thorne in the witness box, had the opportunity of judging the circumstances and assessing the truth for themselves. Perhaps they thought that the natural instinct of an innocent man coming across the dead, hanging body of his fiancée would be to call for help, that it was not rational for him to go through the gruesome dismemberment and burial of the body unless to cover up a terrible crime.

There was one other matter that Spilsbury revealed in his report and that none of the other doctors could dispute. Elsie Cameron was not, and never had been, pregnant.

So, was she deceiving Norman Thorne? Was she trying to blackmail him into marriage? And is it possible that, but for her deception, both she and Norman Thorne might have gone on to lead the decent lives their childhoods had promised?

3

GRUESOME LEFT LUGGAGE

The Murder of Violet Kaye, 1934

Tony Mancini was a "heavy", a tough character who had worked for some of the ruthless racketeers in London's Soho. A former boxer, he once admitted to turning the handle on a meat mincer while his victim's hand was forced into it. On another assignment he had "marked" a "squealer" by chopping off his hand with an axe.

With his swarthy complexion, Mancini might easily have been mistaken for an Italian, but in fact he had been born in 1908 at Newcastle upon Tyne and his given name was Cecil Louis England. Tony Mancini was merely one of several aliases he found useful in his dubious work, which had acquired him a string of minor convictions in London. Among his other "covers" were Antoni Pirille, Luigi Mancini, Hyman Gold and Jack Notyre.

Inevitably he made enemies and there were plenty of people out to get him if they could. After sustaining serious injuries during a brawl at a night club where he was the bouncer, the 25-year-old hard man spent enough time in hospital to reflect on the risks he ran. So it was perhaps not hard for an older woman, 41-year-old Violet Kaye, to persuade him that he was more likely to survive if he moved to join her in Brighton, where she earned her living largely through prostitution. Violet was a tragic figure. One of a family of sixteen, she had behind her a failed marriage and she had given up a once-promising career on the stage as a singer and dancer in favour of selling her still-attractive body. To escape memories of the past and the realities of the present she had taken to the bottle and to occasional doses of morphine.

This unlikely pair of lovers came together to live at lodgings close to the centre of the famous coastal resort some time in 1933.

When Violet entertained her clients, Tony would occupy himself in another room. Afterwards they often checked the money together. There is no doubt that they shared some affection for a time, and Tony was useful to have around as protection, for the world of prostitution has its risks of violence too.

Indeed some pretty ugly customers would call on Violet's services and the couple were forced to move on more than one occasion. Their fragile existence is typified by an incident that happened one day when the couple were strolling along the sea front. Suddenly a young man sprang at Mancini and slashed his face with a razor, then turned to attack Violet. Mancini, though, managed to knock the assailant down and he scurried off.

In March 1934 the couple moved home once more, to a rather seedy basement flat at 44, Park Crescent, a back street between London Road and Lewes Road. Their landlord, Henry Snuggs, knew them as Mr and Mrs Watson and understood that the man was a clothes-presser by trade. He found the couple quite affectionate together and never heard them quarrel.

Other people, though, did comment on Mancini's growing aggression and there can be little doubt that by that spring the attraction of his older companion was beginning to pale. The time she was prepared to devote to her clients irked him, so did her often offensive behaviour while drunk and he recoiled from the disturbing shivering sessions she experienced when trying to shake off the effects of taking morphine.

There may have been other factors at work too. He attracted younger ladies in plenty and one of them, Betty Albright, had told him plainly that she would not continue to see him while he lived with "that woman".

Perhaps also living off the earnings of a prostitute offended his sense of masculinity. At any rate he took a job, as a waiter at the Skylark Cafe in one of the famous archways overlooking the sea. This might seem odd work for a man with his reputation, but in fact he acted also as a bouncer should there be any trouble at the cafe. And the job provided him with a convenient place to meet the younger women who attracted him and the wide number of young male criminals who drifted into his company.

His relationship with Violet ended during May 1934. He told friends that they had parted and that she had left Brighton to take up a good job in Paris. Violet's sister in London, who had been planning to visit her for a holiday, was surprised and disappointed to receive a telegram saying: "Going abroad. Good job. Sail Sunday. Will write. Vi."

Humping a large cabin trunk containing all his worldly possessions, Mancini then moved out of Park Crescent into another basement room at 55, Kemp Street, which was conveniently situated within a stone's throw of the entrance to Brighton's busy main-line railway station. He gave his new landlady the name Jack Notyre, assuring her that the trunk held a weighty collection of books and personal items precious to him.

There he appears to have slept contentedly for some six weeks, the trunk at his bedside. That is, until Sunday, June 17, when the Brighton summer was disturbed by a sensational announcement by the police.

The whole town – Mancini included – was stunned to learn that parts of a dead woman had been discovered in a trunk at the left-luggage office at Brighton station.

The baggage had been deposited there between 6.00 and 7.00 pm on June 6 by an unidentified customer. Within a matter of days it had begun to give off a pungent odour and suspicious members of staff called the law. At Brighton police station, officers who forced the container open had the biggest shock of their lives: wrapped in layers of brown paper tied with a window cord, and packed with a cheap cotton wool, they found a female torso. The head, arms and legs had been hacked off. There were no clothes. The only possible clue to the woman's identity was some neat writing in blue pencil on a sheet of brown paper. All that could be read were the letters … FORD, the preceding part of the word having been completely obscured by dried blood.

Chief Inspector Donaldson and Sergeant Sorrell of Scotland Yard led the full-scale murder hunt that proceeded to occupy the attention of policemen throughout Sussex, much of Britain and other parts of the world for a full twelve months.

At first the hunters were very hopeful of getting quick results. The pathologist Sir Bernard Spilsbury was able to provide a useful profile of the dead woman: well-nourished, light brown hair, aged about 25, 5ft 3½in tall, no body scars, no poison in the stomach, no sign of violence on the body or, on the other hand, any sign that death had been from natural causes. She was four to five months pregnant but had not given birth before. She had been dismembered, by an unskilled hand, shortly after death but there was very little blood in the trunk, so

One of three pieces of luggage recovered by police over the course of several weeks in 1934.

she had probably not been placed in it until well after death. She had died about three weeks prior to discovery, probably in the last week of May.

The nationwide alert that went out swiftly to all left-luggage offices quickly brought results. Three days later a small suitcase deposited at Kings Cross railway station in London was picked out by staff because of its offensive odour. Inside, the police found more gruesome remains: two legs and two severed feet, once more wrapped in brown paper and partly packed in cotton wool, a face flannel, and two copies of the *Daily Mail*, dated May 31 and June 2, 1934. Oddly, the brown paper was soaked in a type of oil.

Spilsbury was able to confirm that the new finds fitted the torso exactly. The feet were well pedicured, suggesting a woman from a middle-class background who had taken pride in her appearance. What he couldn't say was the cause of death, and that might well have been linked to the missing head which railway employees up and down the land continued to hunt for enthusiastically as part of their day's routine.

The search was one of the biggest undertaken in Britain between the two world wars. But the trouble was that hundreds of people became swept along in the enquiry as appeals for information were broadcast far and wide, until the police found themselves submerged by evidence. And in those days there were no computers to sort out the relevant clues.

As a result of the publicity, hundreds of written statements were taken, over a thousand telephone messages were recorded, and thousands of letters were received. No fewer than 800 missing women were reported to Scotland Yard; 730 of these were traced and accounted for. The case histories of the remainder were examined in detail, but none revealed any link with the dead woman.

Chief Inspector Donaldson reported "a daily flood of correspondence from distracted parents, amateur detectives and a good percentage of lunatics". He had to set up a special squad to sift the evidence, doing his best to make the task simpler by creating files for each particular aspect of the crime, such as Brown Paper, Cotton Wool, Empty Houses, Suspects, Missing Persons, Smells, and so on.

He had to admit that the "mass of correspondence and vigorous press enquiries tended to fog those charged with the investigation." Nevertheless his team of detectives did make some progress at various points, only to be brought to a halt at dead ends. They traced, for example, the makers of the trunk and suitcase, both of which were purchased new. But they were cheap, in plentiful supply and the shops that sold them were never identified.

A favoured scenario emerged. Some man of position had formed an association with a young woman resulting in pregnancy. Possible threats of exposure and ruin for the man had led to the crime. The death and transfer to the trunk had probably occurred in a small rented house or bungalow in a country district.

The police searched numerous empty houses and made enquiries about the tenants who had occupied them. Many missing women were found and a whole clutch of "suspects" was produced. A young Hove doctor who befriended young women and who kept a bungalow at Shoreham for bathing parties made a statement. A Brighton yacht owner who had been described by a female witness as having "sadistic tendencies" was kept under surveillance. The woman told how she had been persuaded to remove her clothes while on board while the man, also naked, proceeded to obtain his sexual gratification by killing a chicken in front of her and splattering its blood over himself.

Several men whose names included the letters "ford" were interviewed, without result. But it was, nonetheless, the clue of the blue-pencil writing on the brown-paper packaging that produced the most promising line of enquiry in this extraordinary affair.

Into the police net came Ethel Moysey, a secretary at the Loraine Confectionery Factory in Finsbury Park, London, who had read the newspapers and was convinced that the blue lettering was her work. Her evidence was startling. Part of her job was to return any rejected sweets to the firm's parent company and on the packages of brown paper she used to wrap the rejects she wrote "MELTIS, BEDFORD". Police showed her the original piece of paper, examined her blue pencil and gave her a handwriting test. There seemed no doubt: the blue was identical, the handwriting matched, the firm's stock of brown paper was identical in texture and had been cut into half sheets in exactly the same manner as that found in the trunk. Miss Moysey was sure that the writing was hers.

Detectives interviewed staff at Finsbury Park and at Bedford, where they learned that the brown paper was often re-used for sending on goods to branches – which included a depot in Brighton. All female staff were closely questioned and even those who had left the firm in the previous six months were traced.

From all this a new suspect emerged – a married man who had been associating with a young woman and had appeared worried since June. Police watched him closely and even followed him on a holiday to the Isle of Wight. Later they interrogated closely, him and another man from the same firm. But all to no avail. They failed to link him to the crime.

The riddle of the body in the trunk led to many fanciful theories being expounded in the national press. The *Daily Express* offered a £500 reward for new information. A professional medium presented the police with "clues" clutched from the ether.

In the Brighton area alone, police looked into the files of 24 missing women, toured shops that sold luggage, searched empty premises and spoke to numerous worried people seeking absent relatives. Some 200 officers questioned hoteliers and landladies along the coast. A huge map of the town was divided into sectors so that every property could be systematically searched.

Into this boiling cauldron of detail was dropped the name of Violet Kaye, reported to the police as a missing person by a friend who obviously did not trust Mancini. The report was dutifully investigated but, of course, dismissed – Violet was 42, had given birth before and was a well-known prostitute; she was certainly not the woman from the left-luggage office.

The police did, however, call Mancini into the police station for interview on

July 14, 1934. He told them that his real name Cecil Louis England and that he was aged 26. He said that Violet had simply left him to live with another man, a person he was prepared to name. Speaking with "perfect composure" he went on to prove to the satisfaction of the police that he was working at the cafe when the trunk and the suitcase with their grisly remains were deposited. He then firmly denied the suggestion that he had given away items of female clothing to other women in Brighton.

Apparently satisfied, the police let him go. But, in fact, the officer handling the interview was suspicious of Mancini and a discreet watch was kept on his movements. Police observed his return to work in the afternoon, his energetic activity at a Brighton dance hall in the evening and his return, in the company of two young men, to his lodgings in Kemp Street at 12.30 a.m. But police resources do not allow for non-stop surveillance of all suspects and the hounds were called off for the night.

An experienced crook, Mancini seems to have sensed that he was under scrutiny and to have decided that Kemp Street was no longer a comfortable place to be. He packed his bags and, in the company of his two young friends (no doubt members of the local heavy mob there for his protection), he wandered the streets from 3.00 a.m. to 7.00 a.m. Then he boarded a London-bound train at Preston Park station. He was heading back to the anonymity of London.

He was in such a hurry that he left behind his precious trunk.

Among the many ironies of this complex case was that the trunk-murder team had already made a routine check at 52, Kemp Street. But the owners of the boarding house were away and the police had not searched the rooms.

Now, a painter and decorator who had been called in to give the rooms a face-lift recoiled from the awful smells coming from a cupboard in the corner of one of the now unoccupied rooms. Knowing of the trunk-murder case and the search for the rest of the body, he went straight to the police station.

Detectives arrived at 52, Kemp Street, on Sunday, July 15, confident that they were about to discover the head and arms of their murder victim. The house was, after all, only a minute or two from the left-luggage office. Instead what they found set them another, wholly separate, riddle.

Packed grotesquely inside a putrid cabin trunk, shut behind the doors of the cupboard, was a complete female body. And there was no mystery about her identity. It was Violet Kaye. Dead for at least eight weeks, and rapidly decomposing.

It did not take the police long to discover that the rooms had last been

The basement bedroom at 44, Park Crescent, Brighton where Violet Kaye died.

The Kemp Street boarding house where the trunk was eventually discovered.

occupied by the man they had been watching, but Mancini's trail of false names created confusion enough to give him time to make good his escape. Most of his acquaintances in the town of course knew him as Mancini, the landlady at Kemp Street as Notyre, his previous landlord as Watson. To untangle the deception, Inspector Donaldson turned to the mugshots at Scotland Yard's Criminal Records Office and there he found the photograph he wanted: the man on the run was already known to the police under the name of Jack Notyre.

It was natural enough for the police to assume that they had their killer. Indeed, probably the killer of two women in the same month, for Violet's date of death was established as May 10 and the mystery victim almost certainly died a week or so later. Inevitably, the two cases became linked as one in the minds of the investigators, and indeed of just about everyone else who heard about them.

Brighton and much of Britain had been agog at the discoveries at the left-luggage office in that hot June. Daily the nation had been waiting for news that would solve the riddle – the discovery of the head perhaps, a possible arrest. Now the introduction of a whole new victim turned the case from mere sensation into one of world-wide notoriety.

What would turn up next in old travelling trunks?

A nation-wide hunt began for a ruthless, pathological killer of two females, likely to strike again. The name and description circulated to all police stations was that of Jack Notyre.

When the brutal death of his former mistress was revealed, not even Mancini's dubious friends in Soho could offer him succour. He found himself unwanted and isolated, a hunted man. Within a matter of two days of Violet's rotting remains being found he was in custody, arrested by two astute Kent bobbies, P.Cs. Gourd and Triplow, who had taken the trouble to question a "nervous and hesitant" figure walking the London to Maidstone road near Sidcup at 1.35 a.m. on July 17.

From his very first conversations with police, Mancini firmly denied that he had killed Violet. "I don't know who killed her. As God is my judge, I don't know. I am quite innocent, except for the fact that I kept the body hidden", he told them.

He told police that, on the fateful day of May 10, he had met Violet briefly at the Skylark and noticed that she was under the influence of drink, staggering a little. When he had returned home to Park Crescent that evening there had been no reply to his knock and he was obliged to force a way in through the window. He found Violet lying on the bed with her knees almost touching her chin, clutching at a handful of sheets. She had a handkerchief around her neck and there was blood everywhere. He tried to wake her, but then, in a shocking moment of realization, saw that she was dead. He believed that Violet had been murdered by one of her numerous clients, some of whom he knew to be violent.

Why had he not called the police? That was simple. He feared that there was no chance of him getting a fair deal, thanks to his past criminal activities. The only way out had been to conceal the evidence. Now he was prepared to give the name of the man whom he thought the most likely killer – a man with whom Violet had previously cohabitated.

As his tale unfolded, it became obvious that he had made no real plan to dispose of the body. Instead, he had purchased a trunk for 7s 6d from a stall in Brighton market, put the body inside, and then for the next six weeks or more had simply slept in a bed alongside it.

Other tenants at Kemp Street had often complained about a smell, while the landlady had pointed out that liquids were oozing from the trunk. Mancini had responded by wiping up the seeping body fluids and putting down disinfectant. How he managed to sleep under these conditions was not explained.

Pathologist Spilsbury, who had only recently completed his findings on the remains found at the left-luggage office, was able to be more positive about the cause of death in the case of Violet Kaye. He concluded that she had died following a depressed fracture of the skull, almost certainly inflicted with some considerable violence by a blunt instrument, possibly the head of a small hammer.

The police were elated by the early arrest. They discounted Mancini's story – in those times, when the death penalty applied, a fanciful version of the facts from the accused was always part of the game. Detectives began building up a devastating case against him. The evidence included a collection of his clothes found to be splashed with blood and a hammer recovered from the basement at Park Crescent which was almost certainly the murder weapon. A string of witnesses would testify to his mood of aggression against the dead woman. Mancini himself admitted that he had forged the telegram to Violet's sister.

The prosecution would paint a picture of a man who was part of a seedy criminal world and who actively pursued young women. It was a clear-cut case of a womanizer turned killer who had concealed the crime and, on the verge of being found out, had run to escape responsibility.

Chief Inspector Donaldson was as confident as any detective could be that the police had enough to nail Mancini for capital murder. Trunk murder number one could not be laid at his door, but trunk murder number two was surely sewn up.

Certainly if you had read the national press of the day there would have been no doubt in your mind that Mancini was guilty. At the Brighton magistrates court hearing many of the fifty witnesses attested to his violent nature and to his threats to Violet, while the defence took a most unusual course in revealing his past criminal history in a bid to explain his reason for not volunteering details of the death. Few people would have given him any hope of escaping an appointment with the hangman when the trial began at Lewes Assizes on December 10.

But they had reckoned without the counsel for the defence, Norman Birkett, who began painstakingly to demolish the Crown case.

Through skilful cross-examination of prosecution witnesses he painted a quite different picture of the relationship between victim and accused. They had been on the most friendly and affectionate terms – their landlord at Park Crescent had seen them almost as a perfect loving couple. On May 10, Violet had certainly been frightened, Birkett allowed. But she had been under the influence of drugs and drink and she was frightened not of Mancini but of a client.

The hammer recovered from the basement at Park Crescent, used by tenants for breaking up coal, he dismissed out of hand. The experts found no bloodstains on it and of course it could have been used by any "visitor" to kill. Birkett pointed out that, had Mancini used it, surely he would have simply dumped it off the end of Brighton pier at his leisure.

The case against Mancini looked at its strongest when the prosecution called two of his young women friends – Skylark waitress Joyce Golding and 17-year-old Doris Saville. Golding confirmed that Mancini and Violet had been quarrelling and said that she had visited Park Crescent after May 10 and that Mancini had then given her some of Violet's clothes as a present. She had noticed a shirt with a small bloodstain on it and washed it out for him. Even more damning was the testimony of Saville, who alleged that Mancini had asked her to provide an alibi for him – to say that they had visited Violet at Park Crescent for tea on May 10, had left her alone with three men while going for a walk, and on returning had found her dead.

Birkett threw scorn on this evidence. The so-called quarrels were "wholly false" he maintained, pointing out that Golding's evidence was in distinct contrast to that of other witnesses who had been closer to Violet. As for Saville, he pointed out that she had given very different evidence earlier at the magistrates court. Then she had said that Mancini had told her that he was innocent of murder and that he wanted her help not to cover up murder, but to avoid being wrongly accused.

Seemingly even more serious for Mancini was the evidence of a forensic analyst, Dr Roche Lynch. Roche had examined items of Mancini's clothing and had found blood marks on two shirts, two pairs of trousers and a handkerchief. Blood on one pair of trousers appeared to have spurted from an artery, while marks on one shirt indicated that blood had been splashed on to it. Because of the decomposed state of the body, Violet Kaye's blood group could not be established, so Roche could not say definitely that it was her blood. But surely this was evidence of a killer in action, not of a man who had merely discovered a dead body.

Birkett's reply to this was devastating for the prosecution. He called a tailor, who told the court that, although Mancini had ordered the suit to which one pair of trousers belonged during May, he had not received it until June. He was not in possession of the trousers at the time Violet died. This remarkable revelation began to raise real doubts in the minds of the jury.

But if the splashing and spurting blood had not come from Violet, then whose was it? Because the court was concerned only with Violet's murder, that tantalising question was not asked then and it has never been answered since.

There were other significant triumphs for Birkett as he took control of the proceedings. He got Chief Inspector Donaldson to confirm that the prisoner had nothing to do with the other unexplained trunk murder and that stories in national newspapers alleging that Mancini had been found guilty of previous violent crimes were false. He made the pathologist apologize for failing to inform the defence that a piece of bone from the woman's skull was going to be produced in evidence.

He described his client as "idle, worthless, a man without morals or principles", but not a murderer. Violet, he argued, under the influence of drugs and alcohol, might well have fallen down the steps of the basement flat to her death. He had cast sufficient doubt in the minds of the jury to ask with some confidence for a verdict of not guilty. After deliberating for nearly two and a half hours, the jurors agreed and a bemused Mancini, the man who thought he could never get a fair deal from the law, was freed.

The police were furious about the verdict. The Scotland Yard team had been confident that they had solved one of the two cases that were attracting world-wide attention. Now the hundreds of hours of work that had gone into the two murders had left them with nothing but one unidentified body and one unsuccessful prosecution.

A confidential report written soon afterwards and lodged in the Sussex police files does not conceal the bitterness felt by the investigating team:

How he was able to obtain his acquittal in the teeth of such damning evidence as we were able to bring forward will for ever remain a mystery. What we said about the jury cannot be repeated even here.

You can imagine how greatly hampered we were by having two murders to investigate at one time. It necessitated the utmost care being taken to keep separate the investigations of both crimes, and thus avoid possible confusion in dealing effectively with crime number one.

The correspondence became more voluminous and mystifying because by this time the public in general had made up their mind that the crimes were the work of the same man, and they wrote accordingly with suggestions that were not always helpful.

The investigations into crime number one were continued for many months after the conclusion of the Kaye case – in fact twelve months later we were still answering correspondence, chiefly relating to missing women, but never at any time were we able to obtain the slightest clue as to the identity of the victim or the person responsible – and so one of the most amazing crimes in history has had to be added to the list of unsolved murders.

That was written by a Scotland Yard detective (probably Donaldson himself) with something of a flair for dramatic prose, and it might have provided a suitable end to the affair. But 42 years later there was yet another ironic twist to the tale.

Mancini was living somewhere in the north of England when, nearing the age of 70, he was persuaded to give an interview to News of the World journalist Alan Hart. In it he confessed to killing Violet. Two years later, in an interview with writer Stephen Knight, he repeated his confession and, this time, backed it by swearing an affidavit in which he admits that he and Violet had had a violent row, that he had punched her on the chin and that then in a blind rage he had banged her head on the fender at Park Crescent.

Alan Hart also published a new statement by Mancini's girl friend, Betty Albright. She now claimed that she had seen blood on Mancini's shirt on the day of the murder and that when she had asked him how it had got there he had admitted the killing. This evidence had not been given at the trial.

Two others attracted by the publicity contacted the police with new information. A man from Portslade said that he had heard Mancini bragging about killing a woman soon after the acquittal. A Gloucester man had heard the same boasts

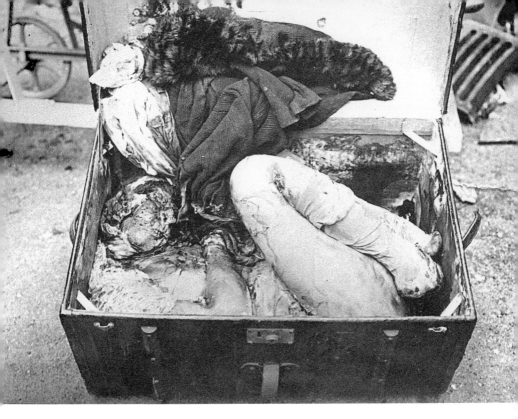

The awful consequences of Mancini's attack. An official police forensic photograph.

from a person calling himself Tony England while serving with the RAF in Gloucester during 1940.

As a result a senior Sussex detective was given the task of re-opening the infamous Brighton Trunk Murders file in 1976. It still contained a gruesome set of photographs taken of both bodies and the 34-page Yard report probably prepared by Chief Inspector Donaldson, but the investigation papers and the original witness statements prepared for the trial had been destroyed in 1964 on the orders of the Brighton police chief.

The Director of Public Prosecutions stated that independent corroboration of Mancini's claim was essential and because of the time elapsed between 1934 and 1976 this would not now be available. In a letter to the Chief Constable of Sussex he finally brought the saga to its end: "My opinion therefore is that there is insufficient evidence available or likely to become available to prosecute Mancini for perjury."

If Mancini's confession in his advanced years was genuine it does settle the case of poor Violet, and of course vindicates the view of Donaldson. But it also makes a mockery of the 1934 trial and the manner in which a clever defence counsel was able to pick holes in what at one time had seemed a cast-iron case.

It is hard not to sympathise with the police. The enquiry was unique. By an uncanny coincidence two killers of women had left bodies in not dissimilar trunks in the same neighbourhood of the same town, within three weeks of each other. The resulting confusion can perhaps be forgiven.

The most puzzling question left to explain is the police failure to identify victim number one, after what was one of the most extensive investigations into missing women ever undertaken. Surely among the mountain of information that poured into Brighton police station from around Britain and other parts of the world during 1934 there must have been a link to the well-nourished 25-year-old who had come from a good family and had taken great care of her appearance?

As to the identity of the murderer, the only clue was that brown-paper packaging with the word "FORD" written in blue pencil. And that trail had come to an end at a confectionery factory.

Perhaps one day someone will do what Mancini did and reveal the answer to this murder mystery. Or perhaps the killer has already gone with his secret to the grave.

4

THE BODY IN THE PARK

The Murder of Joan Woodhouse, 1948

More than 42 years after 27-year-old Joan Woodhouse was found brutally murdered on a lonely hillside, the mystery of her death still stands out among the unsolved crimes on Sussex Constabulary files.

What was she doing on the hillside in the first place? Why was Scotland Yard so slow to recognize the truth? Who raped her, strangled her and then fled the scene? Two of the top detectives of that era undertook separate and extensive inquiries, while a private investigator was called in to add what he could. But none of them solved the riddle.

Joan was an intelligent and independent young woman who earned her living as a librarian. Serious and hard-working, she held strong religious beliefs. Slim, petite and blue-eyed, she was not unattractive, though in her official police description she was given sallow skin, mousey hair, straight nose, oval face, two overlapping front teeth and a mole on her upper lip.

Born in Barnsley in 1921, an only child, she obtained her School Certificate at the Girls High School and studied hard at evening classes before starting work as an assistant at the Barnsley Municipal Library. From there she progressed to the West Riding County Library. She passed her Library Association examinations in 1942 and then won a place at the School of Librarianship at London University.

During the war years she did a spell of national service as a draughtswoman. Later she was released to help her parents run a residential youth club in Barnsley, where her father, Thomas Woodhouse, was the warden. However it was not long before she returned to her books.

Life for her was probably at its most exciting during 1947. In that year she obtained the post of assistant at the National Central Library and moved to work in London for the princely annual salary of £310. In the same year she fell in love with a man of her own age, 27-year-old Edward Roberts, a fellow librarian who came from Folkestone and with whom she shared many interests.

Friends said that they were "very much in love" and looked set to marry. However, early in 1948 their romance ended in a quarrel – apparently over their attendance at a library conference at which Edward was due to speak. Joan was devastated. Suddenly she found herself a very lonely young woman in a big city. It was too much for her to bear; she had a nervous breakdown, came close to suicide and had to resign her job and go to live for several weeks with an aunt, Ida Sheriff, at Bridlington.

Mrs Sheriff and another aunt, Mrs Blades, had always been fond of Joan; they had spent some very happy times in her company when they shared a home in the Sussex coastal resort of Worthing between 1936 and 1940. As a teenager she had spent several memorable holidays with them. Her invalid mother had died in 1943 and since then the two aunts, now both living in Bridlington, had acted almost as substitute mothers. Between them, they coaxed her back to health and in May she was fit enough to return to her job at the London library.

Because of her mental state, her doctor insisted that she should not live alone, so she found accommodation in the company of other young women at the Y.W.C.A. hostel at 29, Bennetts Park in Blackheath. Here she made several good friends and here she appears to have been content. She planned to spend the August Bank Holiday weekend of 1948 in Barnsley with her widower father, with a likely call in at Bridlington as well. Or so it was thought. There was certainly no doubt in the mind of her room-mate, typist Nicole Ashby, that Joan's destination was her father's home in Park Road, Barnsley, when she left the hostel, carrying a blue weekend case, soon after 8.30 a.m. on Saturday, July 31. Several people saw her go – she was not easy to miss because she was wearing what was by 1948 standards a somewhat extravagant blue Paisley frock with yellow and pink stripes.

However, it was not northwards that she went, and to this day no-one has discovered why she did not go direct to the Yorkshire-bound train.

She never arrived in Barnsley. Her father sent a telegram to the hostel asking: "Are you ok? If not, come home. Auntie is worried". Then hostel warden Jessie Maddocks became anxious when Joan did not return after the weekend break and head librarian Miss Feltwell telephoned to find out why she had not arrived for work.

By the Tuesday Joan was a missing person on London police files and a detailed description of her was in general circulation. Her father and her aunt Ida feared that she might have gone away to commit suicide; they came, in a state of great anxiety, to London, and removed all her belongings from the hostel.

It was to be many days before they would learn the full, horrifying story of what had happened to Joan.

On that summer Saturday morning she had, in fact, travelled in the opposite direction to her stated destination, going southward by train into Sussex. What possessed her to do this will never be fully explained, however it is likely that she was still feeling depressed – perhaps suicidally so – and simply wanted to return to a place that held happy childhood memories for her, a place where she had enjoyed summer picnics with her aunts.

At around noon, she deposited her suitcase containing clothing, letters and £7 in cash, at the left luggage office on Worthing Central station, placing the ticket into her brown sling handbag. She is then believed to have boarded a bus to take her ten miles to the picturesque town of Arundel, one of the county's most famous tourist attractions and a place that she loved.

At 2.00 p.m. she bought a bottle of barley water from a chemist's shop in the High Street. She was seen in the Square between 2.00 and 2.30 p.m. by a confident witness. Soon afterwards she set out in her light blue sandals on a long walk past Arundel Castle into Arundel Park, where rolling acres of hills and woods owned by the Duke of Norfolk provide pleasure for many thousands of people every year.

Although she had not been to this spot for some nine years, Joan knew the park very well. Her aunts had often brought her there for picnics and had enjoyed sitting by the beautiful Swanbourne Lake while the lively teenager went off to explore the nearby paths and woods.

Joan must have walked around the shores of the lake, busy and noisy with boaters, and made her way along the rugged footpath which skirts its banks, proceeding for some three quarters of a mile deep into the parkland. About 300 yards beyond the end of the regular path she then climbed up a steep hill and wandered into the thick leafy surroundings of Box Copse which stands at the centre of the park and which, in places, is dense with beech trees and box bushes growing to 15ft or more.

It was a superb summer's day and Joan sat down to sunbathe in a clearing among the trees. She spread her green raincoat on the ground and folded up a fawn lightweight coat to make a pillow for her head. Beside her she placed her bag, the barley water, and a pair of sunglasses. She then removed an artificial pearl necklet – no doubt to get an even tan – and then slipped the multi-coloured dress over her head and placed that alongside her too.

Arundel Park covers an enormous area and only few walkers get as far as Box Copse; even fewer go into it. Joan would have confidently believed that she was well away from prying eyes. Tragically, she was wrong.

An intruder found her there – lying prone in a state of partial undress, revealing her pink camiknickers, brassière, suspender belt and stockings. The startled Joan must have jumped to her feet and tried to escape, but just 12 yards down the bank was trapped by the base of a tree, roughly raped and then brutally strangled.

It was a remote and lonely spot. No-one heard. And the assailant immediately made good his escape, leaving her partly clothed body lying on the ground and the small pile of her possessions where she had neatly laid them out.

Her body and her belongings remained there in the centre of Box Copse untouched and undisturbed for the next ten days – right through the Bank Holiday weekend and through the whole of another weekend, at the peak of a warm summer. Numerous walkers and pleasure seekers must have passed close by, but none entered the clearing.

The grim sight was finally revealed on the afternoon of Tuesday, August 10, when a 24-year-old painter named Thomas Stillwell came scampering down the hill and breathlessly asked Swanbourne Lake lodge-keeper Frank Ferris if he could borrow a bike, because he had found a body.

Stillwell arrived at Arundel police station at 5.20 p.m. and reported what he had seen to Sergeant Bristow who, in the company of another officer, hurried to the copse.

There they found Joan's rapidly decomposing body lying face upwards with legs together, the left knee bent upwards. Further up the sloping ground they found her clothes and belongings, all soaking wet.

Within 24 hours, Guy's Hospital pathologist, Dr Keith Simpson confirmed that it was murder. The victim was a healthy woman, he reported, but, because she was only of medium build, it was unlikely that she had much chance to put

Joan Woodhouse out with
girl-friends in London.

up strong resistance. Death had been caused by asphyxiation through manual
strangulation, by an assailant who had used considerable force.

Before death, she had been subjected to forceful sexual intercourse. Her
stockings were torn and there were bruises on her thighs and a three-inch deep
scratch on one leg. Bruises to the neck and to the back of the head suggested that
she had been pressed down on her back.

Simpson's confident theory was that Joan had been attacked while lying on
her mackintosh, chased a few yards down the slope and then forced to the
ground, where she was sexually assaulted before being silenced for ever.

Suddenly the tranquil little town of Arundel, set picturesquely on the tidal
River Arun, was thrown into the national limelight of a major murder investigation that required the immediate attention of Scotland Yard.

One of the Yard's famed "top five", Detective Chief Inspector Fred
Narborough, accompanied by Detective Sergeant Pattison, came dramatically on

to the stage, confident that he would clear up this simple case in the Sussex countryside with plenty of time to spare before the end of summer.

But this powerful team from the Metropolitan Police, in spite of their great experience of such crimes, made a fundamental error, which sent dozens of policemen looking in the wrong direction. Narborough took one look at the carefully piled clothing in the copse, another at Joan Woodhouse's personal diary found in her bag, and drew the conclusion that this was just another case of a male-female relationship that had got out of hand.

In that diary was a list of around a hundred names and addresses, mostly men, and Narborough was sure that the killer would be speedily prised out from among this considerable circle of friends. Although friends and relatives stressed that men did not figure prominently in Joan's social life, the initial verdict of the police was that, however unpalatable that might be for relatives, the victim had been involved in a secret affair.

A conference of police officers came to the conclusion that she had gone to Worthing with a man friend or had met a man there. The couple had visited Arundel Park on a hot afternoon and she had been partly responsible for any sexual act which subsequently took place.

This fatal appointment with a mystery man became their focal point and, although the body was found at Arundel, it was into the town of Worthing that a team of fifteen police officers surged to begin one of the biggest door-to-door hunts of the post-war years.

This seemed the logical place to start because a cloakroom ticket found in the dead woman's handbag had led detectives to Worthing railway station, where they picked up the blue leather weekend case, neatly packed with clothing.

Every boarding house, hotel and apartment house in the seaside resort was visited by plain-clothes detectives, each carrying a photograph of Joan Woodhouse. They all asked the same question: did this girl book accommodation for herself and a man on the night of July 31? Did the man occupy a bed alone?

The diligent officers obtained the names and addresses of every unattached male who had been staying in Worthing during that weekend. In four days they completed the job, turning their attention next to Arundel and the surrounding villages, where the same two questions were repeated over and over again.

To be absolutely thorough, Narborough insisted on tracing every holiday-maker who had been in Worthing and Arundel on July 31 and had the local police visit them at their homes. Every employee of British Rail at Victoria, Worthing and Arundel was interviewed. The drivers and conductors of coaches between London and the coastal towns were seen. All males over 15 years of age in Arundel were closely questioned in a laborious trail of door knocking.

The meticulous but "discreet" enquiry went even further afield to include students and male associates from Joan's college days, her former fiancé (who accounted for his movements), a male family friend in Edinburgh and the warden of a West London mission who had promised to keep an eye on her.

All this took six weeks. But not a single positive link could be found to tie in with July 31 and the girl in the coloured dress. Eventually, the senior Yard sleuth had to admit that he had exhausted every possible avenue.

Yet there were some simple answers to some simple questions that Narborough had failed to ask at the beginning of his investigation. Now they came to light, and they changed the course of everything.

The hundred names in Joan's diary were all members of the Librarianship Old Students Association of University College, to which she was the honorary secretary. There was no man in her life – apart from her former fiancé, it was books not men that had absorbed her.

In a new interview, Ida Sheriff told the police why she thought her niece had taken off her dress and removed her necklace. It had nothing to do with sex. Joan loved the outdoor life and almost worshipped the sun; she was an obsessive sunbather. "At the first blink of real sunshine she would strip off her outside clothing and lie down", in the back garden or out in the countryside.

Speaking some ten years later to a magazine journalist, Fred Narborough said, sadly:

The events of the fatal Saturday at last became clear. The clarity mocked the six wasted weeks when we hunted a shadowy male companion who had never existed. Instead of seeking a secluded spot for love-making she had gone alone straight to Box Copse, which she knew.

She must have eased her frock over her head, then neatly folded the garment to add to the tidy, growing pile of possessions by her side. The string of pearls would have been unclasped so that the evenness of her suntan around the throat would not be ruined – the throat that was later to feel the grip of the murderer's hand.

As Narborough was forced to go back to square one, a totally different scenario confronted him. He wrote later:

I became satisfied that Miss Woodhouse was of exemplary character, went to the park alone, climbed to this lovely secluded spot where she removed her frock, either to sunbathe or because she was hot, and that she was there gravely indecently assaulted and murdered by a man who was a complete stranger to her.

She was savagely attacked, proof of the rough character of the sexual act. The strangling injuries are consistent with the greatest violence being used, her bestial assailant leaving her to her fate, neither knowing or caring what it would be.

Now, instead of seeking a boyfriend, Narborough was on the trail of an opportunist lurker in the park – a man who had stumbled across the scantily clad figure of the young woman and, in the secluded surroundings of the copse, could not control himself.

The police had already traced several people who had been in the park on the afternoon of July 31, but when Narborough sat down to reconsider the possibilities, one figure began attracting his attention more than the others. It was that of Thomas Philip George Stillwell, the young painter who had first found the body.

A local man born and bred, Stillwell lived with his parents, two brothers and grandfather in a tied cottage at Offham, a hamlet that borders the Arundel estate. The family's landlord was the Duke of Norfolk himself, and the energetic young Thomas knew the land and the park well.

During the war Stillwell had been employed in the docks helping to make Mulberry harbours. At one time he almost became a professional footballer. He earned his money as a painter in the employ of an Arundel builder and was a well known figure in such venues as The Black Rabbit and the General Abercrombie, where he enjoyed the local beer and a game of darts.

A slim 5ft 8in, with long, fair, wavy hair, he was a healthy young man who had a natural interest in the girls of the town and was known to several. In his own words he admitted that he was "a bit hot natured". He had been engaged to a W.A.A.F named Mary Richardson for a time, but she had broken off the relationship just before Christmas 1947, and since then he had not had a regular girl-friend.

Thomas Stillwell had been helpful to the authorities, and had simply given a routine statement to the police on August 11 stating how he had found the body. There had been no good reason to doubt his position, until of course the enquiry began looking in other directions.

Subsequent interviews with witnesses revealed that he had been seen in the park on the day of the murder. Not only that, more than one person believed they had seen him talking to and walking along the path with a young woman who closely resembled the victim.

During further interviews with Detective Inspector Dean of the Sussex police and Sergeant Pattison, Stillwell did his best to explain away this situation. Yes, he had been in the park during the morning and had spoken with two other painters, Frank Clements and Robert Challen, when they had stopped by a walnut tree close to Box Copse. At about the same time he had seen a girl walking about 30 yards ahead towards the copse. After Clements and Challen had moved on, Stillwell said that he walked up the slope towards the copse and saw the girl coming back down the path. As she passed him he had said "Good morning, lovely day", but she made no reply. He went on:

The girl I saw was about 30 to 35 years, dark complexion, swept-back hair and I think she was wearing a dark coat or mac. I did notice that she was carrying a book. I did not notice what shoes she was wearing or whether she had any stockings on. I remember that the coat she was wearing was very long. The photograph shown to me of Joan Woodhouse is similar in face to the girl that I saw. She seemed to be very nervous when I spoke to her, she just seemed to look at me and hurried off.

When Pattison produced a photograph, and began asking questions about it, Stillwell displayed some distress for a moment and then said: "If it was Joan Woodhouse I saw, then I must be to blame for what happened to her". Asked to explain, he replied: "Well, if it was me who frightened her, I expect she ran into the copse where someone found her." He then added: "I don't think that was the girl I saw. She is similar in face and build. That is all I will say."

Of course, if this meeting had taken place during the morning it is highly unlikely that the woman was Joan because she was still travelling down to Worthing then. Nothing more was said to the young man for a whole month while the detectives spent their time checking and collecting detailed statements.

It was on October 19 – more than two months into the investigation – that Narborough decided to play one last card in his frustrating investigation. And that was to call Stillwell in for another, more intensive, round of questioning.

The 24-year-old was called into Arundel Police Station at around 9.30 p.m. to face many hours of interrogation by Narborough and Pattison of the Yard and Detective Inspector Dean and Detective Sergeant J.O. Cowley from Littlehampton. The four officers wanted to know everything about his movements on July 31 and they extracted from him a much more detailed, and sometimes controversial, statement.

Stillwell claimed that the three holiday days of that weekend had been much the same to him and it was difficult to recall precise detail. However, as the long session progressed his timetable on the crucial day of July 31 became clearer.

He was now "pretty certain" that he had not been in the Park during the morning; he had been painting. The visit there during which he had met Challen and Clements and had seen the girl must have been during early afternoon, though he could not put a precise time to it. He had then gone into Arundel to meet the 3.30 p.m. bus to see an office girl named Gwen, but when she did not turn up he had boarded a bus for Littlehampton. In that seaside town he had purchased a shirt from Hepworths, had gone to the cinema, had a cup of tea in the Odeon cafe and then returned to Arundel, where he had played darts for the rest of the evening at Newburghs public house, returning home at about 11.25 p.m.

For the benefit of the detectives, Stillwell repeated his story of seeing the woman on the footpath not far from Box Copse, of saying hello to her but getting no reply. However, he was now less sure that it might have been Joan Woodhouse, and he pointed to numerous other people who had been around at the time, including a group of Girl Guides, another girl who he had seen meeting a man, and a man who had been using field glasses.

"In my last statement I made I said the photograph shown to me of Joan Woodhouse is similar in face to the girl that I saw", he continued. "This may have been the result of the hair style, which seems to give the appearance of a fattish face. I should say that her build appeared to be thickset but that may be as the result of the loose fitting coat."

Then he added: "Although all the facts about this case seem to point to me I am perfectly innocent and have no connection whatever with the death of Miss Woodhouse. This girl I saw on the pathway I do not know who she was but I do not believe it was Joan Woodhouse."

The interrogation ended at around 5.30 a.m. The sum total of this night's work for Narborough was to shift Stillwell's original morning walk in the Park to early afternoon, and that for him was progress.

However, he was little further forward. He had insufficient evidence to make an arrest and no other avenues left to explore and he said as much when the inquest was resumed on November 22 before Horsham coroner Mr F.W.Butler. He also stated emphatically that there was no secret lover and that any insinuations about Joan's character were "completely untrue". (Of course, it had been the police enquiry itself that had provoked these tales in the press.)

The inevitable verdict of "murder by some person or persons unknown" brought the official proceedings to an end and, without any new evidence being forthcoming, it heralded the somewhat ignominious withdrawal of the Scotland

A Sussex police reconstruction showing the clothes Joan Woodhouse was wearing on the day she was murdered.

Yard team, leaving Thomas Stillwell to get back to his life and the community of Arundel to recover its breath.

However, if the police were content to let matters rest there the Yorkshire family of Joan Woodhouse was not. They had been stunned by Joan's death and the manner of it, but they had also been angered by suggestions that somehow she had been free and easy with her affections, a line that had been eagerly followed by some newspapers when they learned of the list of names. Now they became incensed by the failure of the police to catch the offender.

The normally reserved aunts, Mrs Sheriff and Mrs Blades, could not contain their frustrations as a whole year passed without action. On the first anniversary of the murder they made a dramatic pilgrimage south from Bridlington to Arundel and there, on the afternoon of July 31, 1949, made the trek along the path by Swanbourne Lake up to the fringes of Box Copse. Patiently they waited for the anticipated return of the killer to the scene of the crime. They saw nothing suspicious. However there was someone else there watching intently. Sussex police had not overlooked the possibility that a man with certain psychological tendencies might be drawn back. They were under cover, and they watched the aunts come and go.

The two determined ladies returned again in September, this time walking past the cottage where the Stillwell family lived and later attempting to have a conversation with Thomas Stillwell and his mother in the street.

There was nothing to be gained from actions such as these and eventually the two aunts decided on another course. With the agreement of Joan's father they went to see a private enquiry agent in their home town of Bridlington – Thomas Percy Jacks, a member of the British Detectives Association and a former sergeant with the Yorkshire CID.

With the aid of an offer, published in the *News of the World*, of a £500 reward for new information, Jacks set out on a one-man crusade to re-open the case. But from the day that he moved into the St Philip's Guest House in Arundel to begin work it was obvious that his intrusion was not going to be popular, especially with the police.

For a start, the authorities did not favour the idea of a reward. They believed that the Yard enquiry had been "extensive and meticulous" and felt that "financial incentive", so far from producing new, might well result in false information being tendered, thus wasting police time and causing further distress to relatives.

Jacks, undeterred, pressed on. He talked at length with the known witnesses and over a period of months began to compile a whole new dossier. On occasions he claimed to have unearthed "new evidence" and a string of extravagant stories was published in newspapers. One story was about a laundry consignment taken to Stillwell's aunt on August 1 or 2, 1948. The *Daily Mail* made much of that, but police poured cold water on it in a statement to another journal, prompting Jacks to write a wounded letter to Chief Constable R.P. Wilson: "I never wished for press propaganda. They chased me within 48 hours of my arrival. I fully realise that odds were very great against me in solving this serious case, but whilst the felon remains free I would respectfully suggest there is always a chance. I feel that I am performing a public duty although I don't appear very welcome by the police."

This crossfire in the national press was getting out of hand. Even Stillwell joined in. With his solicitor and an uncle, he had a secret meeting with a newspaper reporter in a hotel room, which resulted in the *Sunday Pictorial* running splash headlines on the "local gossip" that was ruining the life of a young man and his new fiancée.

Welcome or not, Jacks actually did pull off a remarkable legal coup. Almost exactly two years after the body of Joan Woodhouse had been discovered, her father and the enquiry agent put into motion the necessary procedure to obtain a warrant for an arrest. It was the first such private application since 1865.

Sitting in private session on Wednesday, August 30, 1950, magistrates at Littlehampton listened at length to testimony from five witnesses and what they heard led them to sanction the arrest of Thomas Philip George Stillwell, on a charge of murder.

What the might of Scotland Yard had shirked was now achieved by private means. The once-reluctant Director of Public Prosecutions was obliged to take over the prosecution, instructing Mr J.S. Bass as counsel. Similarly, the Yard was obliged to re-activate its interest and, with Narborough in retirement, they called in the famous Detective Superintendent Reginald Spooner to begin a third investigation into the murder.

Stillwell continued adamantly to deny the charge. When Inspector Dean called for him at Offham, he said simply: "There is only one thing to say, I am innocent." This time it was not for a cosy chat, but remand in custody inside Brixton Prison.

Fortunately the police and the magistrates at Arundel were able to stage the preliminary hearing quickly, for much of the necessary groundwork had already been completed earlier by Narborough. In less than three weeks, on September 9, Stillwell was brought before Arundel Magistrates Court, where a bench sitting in public spent four days listening to the evidence of thirty-five witnesses.

By now, of course, the evidence was old, the memories of people in the park on the relevant days less sharp. The picture that was presented was confusing and there was more than one discrepancy in dates offered to the court.

Key witnesses were muddled. Clements said that the meeting with Stillwell in the Park was between 9.30 and 11.00 on the morning of July 31. Challen said it was between 2.00 and 4.00 in the afternoon. Another witness, Mrs Nelly Petley, told the court that she had asked Stillwell for the time while walking in the park close to Box Copse, and that he was with a woman who resembled Joan Woodhouse. However the prosecution had great difficulty in establishing a firm date for this crucial meeting, and defence solicitor Mr V.H.O. Jackson was quick to exploit the situation.

Even the prosecuting counsel admitted that the evidence against the defendant was "wholly circumstantial" and that there was no direct evidence to show that he was party to a crime. "You will therefore want to examine the evidence that is available, and you may consider from that evidence that it shows no more than that he had the opportunity to commit this crime if he so desired", he told the bench wanly.

One of the strangest pieces of evidence was a dart that had been discovered in the vicinity of Box Copse soon after August 10, some 45 feet away from the murder scene. It was clean and in bright condition, suggesting that it had not been there long. It naturally provoked much attention from the many observers who commented on the case. Stillwell made no secret of the fact that it was his – indeed he had reported it missing to Arundel police and had shown them the remainder of the set. He often kept three darts in the top pocket of his jacket and believed that one had fallen out on the day he had stumbled across the body. Detective Inspector Spooner, in his final report on the case, said that he was quite content to believe this to be the truth of the matter.

During his final address on behalf of Stillwell, Mr Jackson stressed the discrepancies over dates, times and sightings and the lack of evidence. He told the bench:

I say therefore that some man got in touch with this woman and got into violent sexual intercourse with her. But who that man was we do not know. This case has been going on for two years and now has come this very great strain upon the accused. He has been in custody since the end of August and I ask you to remember that if he is committed he will have to wait months for trial.

These have been weeks of horror for him and I ask you to say that there is no evidence at all that he was the man who murdered this woman on July 31, 1948, and that there is no case to answer.

After a two-hour adjournment, chairman Mr E.M. West announced the decision of the Bench: "We have carefully listened to the evidence over the last three days, and we are of the unanimous opinion that there is not sufficient evidence to justify sending the case for trial and we therefore direct that you, Thomas Philip George Stillwell, be discharged from this court."

Now, of course, the suspect was the victim. Although he was permitted to return to the anonymity of his painting in Arundel, what amount of stigma would stick to him and for how long? The defendant who goes for trial and wins can at least go away with a "not guilty" verdict for his consolation. In the rare event that a magistrate will not commit for trial, it is simply a question of a discharge from the court.

The Director of Public Prosecutions could certainly argue that he had been right all along not to proceed, while the two distinguished Yard men, Spooner and Narborough, could only sit back and wonder where they had gone wrong.

Spooner had traced Joan Woodhouse's life in some detail. He found her to be something of a lone figure, with no men friends, and thought that she may have been going through a period of conflict over her religious beliefs. He is said to have developed a private theory that Joan simply laid down in Box Copse to commit suicide with sleeping tablets (a single tablet of luminal was found in her bag).

In his memoirs, Narborough reveals that the case played on his mind for years afterwards. "To this day I look back in anger on the tragedy of Box Copse," he was quoted as saying in 1959. "Down the years I have waited for a man to make his mistake. To take a drink too many, perhaps, and talk too loudly...".

Such hopes were never realized, but this is a case that has refused to die. During the following 30 years numerous people have come forward to state categorically that they knew who did it, or even to "confess" to the killing of Joan Woodhouse. Why quite so many have felt this urge is itself uncanny.

Sussex detectives say they are baffled by the phenomenon. Other murders happen without so much as a whisper from anyone, yet in the case of the Arundel Park riddle the file of suspects provided by "helpful" citizens and those ready to "own up" has to be seen to be believed.

There was the prisoner awaiting execution at Exeter, the Yugoslavian refugee described as a "sexual neurotic", an unemployed piano tuner, the former Sussex man who had written a suicide note in South Africa, a welder with "maniacal tendencies", the British Rail cleaner who told a sergeant "I done the girl at Arundel", a housebreaking suspect found with a confessional note, a former Navy dental surgeon, a United States serviceman, and even a German prisoner-of-war supposedly in custody somewhere in Sussex. The claims continued to roll in regularly from 1949 until 1969 with one as recent as 1980.

Some of them came from distraught wives determined to inflict harm on unfaithful husbands. Some were from people with known psychiatric disorders. A few were clearly from sources who genuinely believed they had stumbled on new evidence. All have been investigated and eliminated.

Of course, mystery breeds speculation and this does appear to be destined to remain among those tantalising cases that are never solved.

Thomas Stillwell continued to live in Arundel and remained in steady employment until he retired. He always strongly denied any involvement in the crime.

It must have taken a special strength of character to face the whole might of the legal system, on a charge that, in those days, carried the death penalty.

He received no legal aid. The court awarded him 40 guineas towards his costs as some compensation for the ordeal that he had gone through, while a national newspaper did a bit better than that with £200 for his story. Taken together, that was not quite enough to pay his solicitor's bill of £249.

5
FRIDAY THE THIRTEENTH
The Acid-bath Murders, 1944-49

If it were ever necessary to compile a top ten of Sussex murderers, the name that would stand out head and shoulders above the rest would be that of John George Haigh.

The Haigh story is not just one of murder. It is also one of forgery and deception on a gigantic scale. He was among the foremost con men of the century. He fooled lawyers, bankers, policemen, sensible businessmen, factory owners and engineers. He deceived his closest friends and even from the young woman who was his constant friend for five years he managed to hide his true nature. Years later that woman remains stunned by what happened. "I never once saw the evil side of him", she admits. "No-one did. That part of him remained totally hidden. I still don't understand how such a thing could happen."

Just how many people he killed was never satisfactorily established. The Scotland Yard tally is six; Haigh himself readily confessed to nine, although in one of his numerous letters written from prison to friends he said that "it could have been a dozen or more".

When he was finally brought to justice, Haigh was declared to be sane – sane enough to stand trial and sane enough to hang. But by any common-sense standards he was certainly unbalanced and the origins of his disturbed mentality can be traced back to his early family life.

C

From the day that he was born in the Lincolnshire village of Stamford in 1909, and throughout his formative years when the family lived in the Yorkshire community of Outwood, near Wakefield, John Haigh was brought up under the repressive regime of the sect of Plymouth Brethren to which his parents belonged. He was denied sport and entertainment. Newspapers and radios were banned. What books appeared on the shelves centred on the religious beliefs of the adults. If a story was to be read, it came from the Bible. Other children did not figure in his life. And if he dared mention the pleasures that he observed elsewhere, he was warned by his father that they were temptations of the Devil.

While this was a strange world, there is no doubt that his parents wanted the best for their only son. They gave him a sound education, first at Wakefield Grammar School, where he shone at divinity and science, and later at the Wakefield Cathedral school where his fine treble voice was appreciated and where his keyboard talents earned him the post of assistant organist.

He become something of a preacher among the local Brethren, and by the time he was a teenager he could debate issues from the Bible with some authority. He seemed to be a model young man destined for a fine career.

But at some point the young Haigh began to rebel against the lifestyle and the teachings of his parents. No-one noticed the mental torment that was un-doubtedly going on inside his mind. And that was because he kept it secret, concealing it beneath a protective veneer of charm. He found that telling lies was often a good means of avoiding an unpleasant confrontation. He discovered too that he had a special ability to forge other people's handwriting, at first copying the signatures of pupils at school.

By his early twenties he was well-spoken, well-dressed and well-groomed and he had held down a string of genuine jobs in Wakefield and Leeds which brought him a steady income.

The moment when he turned towards serious crime came in 1931, when he was 22. The petty cash box at an insurance firm he worked for went missing. Whether he was responsible for the theft is not known, but he was suspected and asked to leave. That dismissal set him on course for a lifetime of crime. The English newspapers were at the time full of reports about a spectacular trial in France, the case of Maître Sarret, a lawyer who had attempted a gigantic insurance fiddle and had disposed of his victim's body in an old tin bath of acid. Haigh had been deprived of newspapers as a child, now he took a great deal of notice of them, and was easily impressed.

At first he contented himself with simple insurance frauds, but he soon became

John George Haigh

bolder and it was, probably, through more ambitious cheating that he acquired enough money to make him a very fashionable man-about-town, complete with flashy red sports car.

Among the many attractive young women drawn to his side was a 21-year-old mannequin from Stockport named Betty Hamer. With promises of a splendid life for them both, he swept her off her feet and they married secretly at Bridlington register office on July 6, 1934. Although they never divorced, it was a relationship destined to survive only four months as Haigh's private life of trickery was suddenly exposed.

The fraud squad arrived at his Leeds office in October wanting to know all about some rather peculiar hire-purchase transactions. Through a series of carefully drafted newspaper advertisements he had posed as a potential garage purchaser, which made it possible for him to obtain, by deceit, a supply of hire-purchase forms from a finance company. He used the forms, and his forging skills, to apply for loans for fictitious car purchases in a variety of names plucked from a telephone directory. He persuaded two young friends to join him in the fraud, and the cheques came rolling in.

But it was a crude fraud. The police arrested all three conspirators, and at Leeds Assizes in November, 1934, 25-year-old Haigh, as the ring-leader, was sentenced to fifteen months in his home-town jail at Wakefield.

The sentence was a tough one, but Haigh was not deterred by it. Indeed, the evidence is that his three periods in jail taught him a great deal about criminals and their methods, and also gave him the opportunity to learn about law and chemistry from a stream of instructive books borrowed from prison libraries.

On his release from Wakefield, he made a final break from Yorkshire and went to work for a wealthy West London family – 62-year-old Donald McSwan, his 57-year-old wife Amy and their 26-year-old son William, or Mac, who owned and ran two lucrative pinball arcades in the Wimbledon area. Haigh was taken on as secretary and chauffeur, and soon became a close companion to Mac.

Haigh left the McSwan's employ after one year to set up business on his own, this time with even bigger fraudulent ambitions in mind. He invented three legal practices with fictional names and addresses: Kenneth Elliott of Chancery Lane, Sanders and Co. of Hastings and William Cato Adamson of High Street, Guildford, Surrey. Then he pored over records at Companies House, ordered large stocks of stationery and had 450 circular letters prepared by a duplicating bureau in Central London. On Saturday, June 4, 1937, shareholders across Britain received an offer from a solicitor who was disposing of a large number of shares at advantageous prices. In a matter of days, money began to pour into the three offices from buyers only too eager for a bargain. In the first week, cheques for £1,050 came in.

Haigh's idea was to hide behind a smokescreen of false names and then to vanish with the money. It might have worked, but for a simple typing slip on one set of circulars. The typist left out the "d" in Guildford and an eagle-eyed shareholder, thinking that a lawyer would not make such an error, reported the discrepancy.

Once more the fraud squad pounced, and at Surrey Assizes on November 23, 1937, Haigh pleaded guilty to obtaining money by false pretences. The judge sent him to Dartmoor to spend four years hard labour for what he called "as bad a case of false pretences as I have yet tried."

When the authorities agreed to release him early on licence on August 13, 1940, he was 31. The veteran of two substantial sentences, he emerged from the bleak fortress on the moor to face a Britain at war.

He could have settled for a new career in the army with many of Britain's young men, and his call-up papers did in fact follow him around, though somehow he never seems to have attended the medical. In his old haunts around the Victoria area of London he did assist the war effort to a degree as a £3-a-week fire-watcher. But in less than a year he was back in trouble. Never one to miss an opportunity to buy and sell, he offered to get a good price on a fridge for his Italian landlady. But the woman claimed that he short changed her and impetuously complained to the nearest police station. Haigh was still on licence from Dartmoor and the hand of the law was heavy. On June 10, 1941, the County of London Sessions sentenced him to another 21 months with hard labour. He was sent this time to Lincoln Prison, which he called the worst jail he had ever known and where the warders "belonged to a race alien to all the men I have ever known".

It was here that the fraudster turned into a scheming killer, and it was here – under the noses of the warders he despised – that Haigh began plotting his new career in murder.

He devoured technical and legal books in the prison library, among which were almost certainly scientific publications on the use of acids. When they offered him the chance to work in the tinsmith's shop he took it eagerly and there he found it simple enough to hold back small amounts of the sulphuric acid used in the routine treatment of metals. From the prison kitchens he acquired a collection of jam jars and by offering tobacco to "trusties" who worked in the fields outside, he obtained a good supply of dead field mice. When the backs of the warders were turned, he would fill the jars with acid, drop the small bodies in and watch fascinated as they disintegrated. He found by these experiments that a field mouse, if immersed in its own volume of cold, concentrated sulphuric acid, will decompose completely. Not even the skeletal remains can survive.

When he left Lincoln in September 1943 he could hardly wait to begin using that formula on human beings.

In order to set himself up with some new finance, Haigh once more set out to find some legitimate work and a newspaper advertisement drew him into Sussex for the first time. He got the job of book-keeper and salesman to a small light-engineering firm in Crawley and took lodgings in Northgate Road.

There is no doubt that Haigh loved this part of Sussex. He eventually came to live, on and off, at the splendid George Hotel in the High Street, became very familiar with a string of skilled men involved in engineering workshops and struck up a firm friendship with a local girl named Barbara Stephens, meeting her nearly every weekend. He virtually adopted Sussex as a second home and retained these links for the remainder of his life.

But, for his criminal career at this stage, he needed the anonymity of London, to which he returned early in 1944. There he took lodgings at Queen's Gate Terrace in Kensington, creating from that bed-sitter another new company, grandly entitled Union Group Engineering, whose headed notepaper boasted branches in Crawley and Croydon. He called it a specialist consultancy. His title was liaison officer.

In reality, he was the sole director and only employee and the company's only assets were one leather briefcase with the initials J.G.H. engraved on the flap, a small secondhand typewriter and the lease on a basement at 79, Gloucester Road, a few minutes stroll from his lodgings and directly opposite the Metropolitan and District Railways tube station.

This rather gloomy cellar was spartan, but it did have several rooms, and it was totally hidden from prying eyes. Here Haigh gathered together the materials he needed, including a substantial stock of sulphuric acid, kept in glass carboys placed in metal containers and packed with straw.

In a London still in the grip of war, its streets blacked out at night, Haigh began a patient search for his first victim. Then, by chance, in the late summer of 1944, he met up again, in the bar of the Goat public house in Kensington High Street, with William McSwan. Eight years had gone by since the two men had worked together for the McSwan family pinball arcades in Wimbledon. Haigh was delighted to renew this friendship with a man of considerable means, and his thoughts must have been racing when his smartly dressed friend informed him that he was thinking of "disappearing" for a while in order to avoid call-up to the army.

The two began to meet regularly. Haigh learned that the McSwan family had sold their arcades and invested the family fortune in five London houses from which they earned very useful weekly rents. Consequently, they needed somewhere to store their redundant pinball machines. Without hesitation, Haigh offered Mac the use of his basement workshop and the "services" of Union Group Engineering.

On the evening of September 9, 1944, the two men met at the Goat. Then, warmed by a bar meal and glasses of wine, they walked through the dark London streets to the basement in Gloucester Road. There it is likely that Haigh waited for a moment until Mac's attention was distracted, then picked up a large piece of lead piping and struck savagely from behind. Mac fell unconscious on the ground and died within minutes.

Now Haigh had not a mouse but a human body to dispose of. For one night he left the body of his former business associate and friend inside the locked cellar. Next day, a Saturday, he was very busy indeed. He took from the body everything of value including the keys to Mac's flat and other personal belongings. He spent a long time forcing the body into an old oil drum that had been used on a nearby bomb site as a water butt. Then, suffering considerable discomfort from fumes, he used a bucket to transfer around ten gallons of sulphuric acid from the carboys to the drum.

That done, he clamped a lid down on the container and left the acid to do its work. He had calculated that a human body would disappear in two days, and although his scientific theories were never perfect, this time he seems to have got it right.

On the Monday, perfect murder number one was completed. Haigh returned to the reeking cellar and during a lengthy and most unpleasant "disposal" exercise succeeded in tipping the gruesome contents of the drum down a drain in the centre of the floor, from where they would slide away into the sewers and, ultimately, the River Thames.

The full deviousness of Haigh's mind now began to become apparent. With Mac gone for ever, he made a friendly call on his victim's elderly parents, Donald McSwan and his still sprightly wife Amy. At their modest Pimlico flat he told them that their son had gone to live in Scotland for a while, to escape national service, and that he could help them run their business by collecting the rents for them.

To sustain the charade, he went regularly to Glasgow and there wrote a series of chatty letters and postcards to the parents, perfectly forging Mac's handwriting and signature. Not once did they suspect him. Indeed, they considered him a very close family friend and in Mac's absence actually did agree to appoint him as their official rent collector.

Haigh had stolen all their son's personal possessions but he wanted the really big prize – the five McSwan properties. So, on the morning of Friday, July 6, 1945, there were two new 40-gallon oil drums standing on the stone floor of the Gloucester Road basement. Haigh never did have any difficulty persuading people to do things for him. By suggesting that Mac was about to return to London, he lured the unsuspecting Donald McSwan down to the cellar and killed him in much the same way as he had killed his son. Amy, told a similar story, was brought to the basement an hour or so later and killed with an iron bar. Side by side their bodies were placed into the drums.

While the rest of Britain celebrated the end of the war, Haigh flushed their dissolved remains down the sewers. He told their friends and neighbours that they had emigrated to America at short notice, and that he had been given power of attorney to deal with their affairs.

During the following weeks he put his talent for forgery to good use. He disposed of all the family's personal effects, then sold off their five houses in deals which even conveyancing solicitors did not question, thus raising himself something in the region of £6,000, which in those days was a small fortune.

Between 1945 and 1947 Haigh lived the life of a lord. He became a permanent resident of the Onslow Court Hotel in Kensington, indulged himself in lavish business enterprises which clearly impressed others, bought himself fine clothes from the London shops, enjoyed the theatre, the ballet and fine music, and was never without a high-powered, flashy car.

It seems that he had hoped to make a genuine success of an engineering business, perhaps by marketing a new product which would sweep the country and make a fortune, but none of his ideas brought success, and by the August of 1947 he was £25 overdrawn at the bank and in difficulty.

At about this time he closed the Gloucester Road basement, having found what he considered to be a much more suitable place for his activities in his favourite Sussex haunts. Among the numerous business partnerships he had formed thanks to the McSwan legacy was one with Edward Jones, owner of Hurstlea Products at West Street, Crawley. The two of them had begun work on developing a revolutionary needle-threading device. Jones had given Haigh permission to use a small workshop in Leopold Road in the same town that he owned but no longer used. To here, late in 1947, Haigh gratefully moved Union Group Engineering and its unique set of equipment.

The premises at Leopold Road were not nearly as private as the Gloucester Road basement. There were houses nearby. Anyone would see comings and goings. But Haigh was by now very confident about his methods.

During the same year he had struck up a new friendship with the charming Dr Archie Henderson and his wife Rose. Archie, aged 52, was a former army medical officer and Rose, more than ten years younger, was a former beauty queen. The couple were wealthy members of London society.

Haigh had worked his way into their circle by purporting to make an offer for their house in Ladbroke Square, West London. In fact, he couldn't possibly afford it and did not buy, but he ended up attending house parties arranged by the Hendersons and playing the baby grand in their lounge for their entertainment.

Giles Yard and the storeroom at Leopold Road, Crawley. A casual comment by Hurstlea's proprietor led D.S. Heslin here when the routine inquiry seemed at an end.

March 1, 1949. Police investigators and a forensic team start to investigate the yard at Leopold Road. Dr Keith Simpson found vital clues here which confirmed the identity of Haigh's last victim.

Eventually he became quite close to Archie, persuading him to invest in a new powder-compact project that he believed would sweep the market. The doctor was won over totally, but Haigh needed to be very patient and had to wait until early in 1948 before an opportunity arose to lure the Hendersons into his carefully prepared trap.

That chance came when the couple decided on a short winter break from London, spending a few days at Broadstairs followed by a weekend at the Metropole hotel on the sea front at Brighton.

At Leopold Road, Union Group Engineering were re-stocking with enthusiasm: three glass carboys of sulphuric acid were brimming full, a brand new stirrup pump had been purchased, there were a pair of rubber gloves on the workbench, a large rubber apron, a heavy raincoat, thigh-length rubber boots, and two very recent acquisitions – a war-time gas mask in its box, and a .38 Enfield revolver hidden in a leather hat-box. Both war souvenirs owned by Archie, and both had been stolen by Haigh from the Hendersons' flat while they were away.

On the pretext of wanting to discuss the powder-compact venture, Haigh invited himself to have coffee with the Hendersons at the Metropole on the morning of Friday, February 13, 1948. He then persuaded Archie that it would be useful to visit his Crawley workshop for a few hours. The doctor agreed. Rose was persuaded to remain behind with their red setter Pat.

The bright red Lagonda with Haigh at the wheel came powering into the picturesque Crawley High Street at just before mid-day. He and Archie apparently enjoyed a very jovial lunch at the George. At about 2.00 p.m. they made the short trip to Leopold Road, where the car was parked inside two heavy wooden gates which enclosed an area of land known as Giles Yard.

Henderson found himself inside a small shack, grimy, untidy and cobwebbed, hardly the place to inspire a money-spinning business deal. Nevertheless, his companion was so persuasive that he was encouraged to look through a sheaf of drawings that had been carefully laid out for his benefit on a workbench. While he was thus preoccupied, Haigh took the gun from the hat-box, turned, positioned the gun a matter of inches away from the neck of his partner and pulled the trigger. Henderson must have died instantly, his body crashing down onto the floor, his skull shattered.

The rest of that Friday the Thirteenth was one of the busiest of Haigh's life. He bound Henderson's body with twine so that the arms were strapped to the torso and the legs pulled up in what he called "turkeywise" fashion. Then, with what must have been considerable effort, he cajoled the heavy body into the waiting oil drum.

Few murderers in history have displayed the coolness and determination possessed by Haigh. He returned to the Metropole hotel early in the evening with another carefully rehearsed fraud for the ears of Rose Henderson.

On the pretext that Archie had been taken ill and wanted to see his wife immediately, he succeeded in luring her from the warm hotel out into the wintry night and back to Leopold Road, supposedly to collect her husband's briefcase before being re-united with him at the house of a nearby friend.

The beautiful Rose often spoke in derogatory terms about John, a man she evidently did not fully trust, but clearly she did not suspect anything sinister about him, so convincing was his tongue. She died in the same manner as her husband, despatched with a single bullet from the same revolver.

Just before midnight, Haigh telephoned the Metropole, posing as a woman, to inform the management that Mrs Henderson would not be returning that night. He asked a porter to make sure that her red setter was taken care of, and "please take him for a walk in the morning".

Haigh enjoyed a good night's sleep in Kensington, but was back in Crawley early on the Saturday to deal with the two bodies. He had learned a lot through disposing of the McSwans, and he believed that his methods had reached a point of near perfection when it came to the turn of the Hendersons.

The gun, of course, was a big improvement for him. The rubber raincoat, boots and gloves would protect his skin from likely splashes from the sulphuric acid. The gas mask would prevent him choking on the deadly acid fumes. The stirrup pump with its length of rubber hosing would make the job of transferring the acid from carboy to oil drum far safer and much less arduous. At Leopold Road, in fact, he had perfected a safe and secure system of which he felt duly proud. Having filled each drum, he simply removed his protective clothing, returned each piece of equipment to its allotted place in the workshop, clamped lids on the drums and left the bodies of his friends to disintegrate.

This time there was no convenient drain into which he could pour the residue, so when he returned to examine his handiwork four days later he tipped the contents of each container over the rubble-strewn land outside the workshop. The black, sludgy liquid simply merged into the flotsam of building materials, stones and shrubs that littered the yard.

The Hendersons had vanished, for good. Haigh paid them one final tribute by writing the initials AH and RH in his diary, next to which he drew the sign of the cross.

Undoubtedly he took considerable pleasure in perfecting this rare method of killing and disposing of evidence, and had become quite sure in his own mind that he could go on cheating the law as and when he chose. But, of course, his real objective was to keep his fine lifestyle going and now firmly in his sights were the lucrative possessions of the Hendersons.

He got the lot – their clothes, furniture, personal effects, a block of flats and a busy London toy shop. Not to mention Pat the red setter, which became his constant companion for many months. This was an amazing accomplishment, impossible to carry off without a high degree of legal knowledge, organization and sheer effrontery. Yet Haigh managed to get away with it, in spite of the close, suspicious attentions of other members of the Henderson family, especially Rose Henderson's brother Arnold Burlin, a Manchester hotelier, who constantly scrutinized his activities. Burlin was an astute businessman, not one easily fooled. Yet even he was taken in.

First Haigh produced a letter of authority supposedly signed by Archie giving him rights to the Hendersons' possessions. He then concocted a story that the Hendersons had agreed to sign over their properties to him in the event that they could not repay a £2,000 loan he had made to them. All this was supported by documentation which lawyers verified.

Probably Haigh's greatest feat of forgery came when he wrote a series of highly convincing letters in the distinctive hand of Rose informing Arnold Burlin that she and Archie were having marriage difficulties and had decided to emigrate to South Africa to start a new life. Their "good friend" John was authorized to handle everything in London and to become owner of their properties in view of his kind loan.

Of course, Burlin was distressed that they were not calling personally to say farewells, and often wondered why they could not leave a telephone number. However, so perfect was the forging of the handwriting and so knowledgeable was the writer about the family's affairs, that he was totally convinced of the authenticity of the letters, and thus of his sister's safety.

There were several tense face-to-face confrontations between Burlin and Haigh, but the smooth talking con man answered every question in convincing style. At one point, the brother was poised to call in the police, but true to form, Haigh quickly blocked that by telling Burlin that Archie had been involved in an illegal abortion and that if the police were involved it could be serious trouble for him. It was, of course, another lie. And one that could not be checked.

In June 1948 Haigh became the legal owner of the shop and flats, and in a matter of months he had turned all the couple's assets into a second windfall worth £7,771.

But evidently his spending needs were becoming more frantic. While it had taken him two years to dispose of the McSwan money, he needed only six months to fritter away the Henderson fortune on his grand lifestyle, the pursuance of business ideas, and the newly acquired quest of trying to raise a quick fortune through betting on horses and the dog tracks of London.

In the January of 1949 he found himself broke for the second time, and naturally he turned to the waiting acid bath at Leopold Road to provide him with another much-needed injection of funds.

Into his sights then moved Mrs Olive Durand-Deacon, a 69-year-old resident of the Onslow Court Hotel. Wealthy, intelligent and attractive, she was described by the manageress as "possibly our best client, impeccable, familiar to everyone and friendly". Her friendships had included John Haigh, whose regular table in the dining room was next to hers. Through this regular meeting point they had been drawn into many conversations over a period of some four years.

It must have seemed like manna from heaven when on Monday, February 14, 1949, Olive put to Haigh an idea she had for manufacturing a new range of plastic fingernails. She had the money to invest in such a scheme and he had the factory and the engineering expertise. They agreed on a little private enterprise together.

Later that evening inside Room 404 he wrote out a rather unusual shopping list, which was later read by police – drum, enamelling brush, H_2SO_4, paint brush, stirrup pump, gloves, apron, rags, cotton wool, some red paper. For two days he busied himself shopping and by Thursday he was satisfied. Inside the Leopold Road workshop stood a new 45-gallon oil drum and alongside it three glass carboys brimful of sulphuric acid.

Haigh and Olive agreed to meet just after lunch on Friday, February 18, to go down to the Crawley workshop. Haigh went to some elaborate lengths to make sure they weren't seen together. He picked her up in his maroon Alvis outside the Army and Navy Stores in Victoria and then, complete with samples of artificial fingernails, they set off for Crawley supposedly to explore the potential of their little scheme.

Her trust in the 39-year-old businessman and fellow resident was obviously total. Dressed in her favourite Persian lamb fur and quite an array of expensive jewellery, the immaculate Mrs Durand-Deacon stepped over the threshold of the grimy workshop at around 4.30 pm on that winter's afternoon with no hint of apprehension or fear.

The order for sulphuric acid collected by Haigh just days before Mrs Durand-Deacon disappeared.

Just as she was bending over to concentrate on some sheets of red cellophane paper that had been carefully laid out on a workbench for her benefit, her companion moved swiftly to the corner of the room to open the lid of waiting leather hat-box on which the initial H was ornately carved. With astonishing speed, Haigh clasped his Enfield revolver into his gloved right hand and, before Olive had any chance to realize what was happening, fired a bullet into the back of her head. There was an instant spurt of blood which sent a spotted spray of red across part of the white-washed wall before the body crashed to the ground.

Haigh stripped the body of its valuables — ear-rings, a diamond wrist-watch,

Mrs Olive Durand-Deacon

a selection of expensive rings, a pearl necklace and a gold crucifix. Then he took from her red handbag 30 shillings and a fountain pen. The valuable fur coat he also kept. Anything he didn't want he simply tossed into the waiting drum, ready for incineration.

Fifteen minutes after the killing he was chatting to his business partner Edward Jones at nearby West Street, where the two men often worked together. At 6.00 p.m. a local van driver came into the yard at Leopold Road to park his vehicle for the night while Haigh calmly got on with the task of moving valuables into his Alvis.

The body was out of sight, packed tightly into an oil drum.

At 6.30 p.m. Haigh was in the Ancient Priors tea house in Crawley High Street having a poached egg on toast. Then he spent a very energetic two hours dressed in his rubber garb and gas mask pumping ten gallons of sulphuric into the tank that held his former dining-room companion. With that job done, it was off to the George Hotel for dinner, followed by a sound night's sleep at the Onslow Court.

No doubt his warped mind thought that this was a good job carried out very much according to plan. But murder number six, though handled with even more ruthless efficiency than any of the others, never reaped the financial rewards that he wanted, and it turned out to be his last.

By selling the gems he raised a mere £110, when they were worth much more. The valuable fur he left at a dry-cleaning shop in Reigate hopefully to be sold in mint condition at a later date. There is no doubt that he had his eyes set on acquiring Mrs Durand-Deacon's small personal fortune of £36,000 tied up in shares and investments. But this time he was stopped in his tracks.

No-one had reported the McSwans or the Hendersons missing, but Olive Durand-Deacon's absence from her hotel did not go unremarked. After fretting for nearly two days over Olive's failure to return, her best friend and fellow hotel guest Mrs Constance Lane decided to report the matter to Chelsea police.

Haigh learned of Mrs Lane's intentions over breakfast at the hotel. Confident even then of his immunity from discovery, he offered to accompany her to the police station, took her there in his car and in front of a duty sergeant began playing the role of an innocent friend anxious to help settle this little mystery.

He nearly got away with it again. But at last the pendulum had begun to swing against him.

The woman police sergeant, Maude Lambourne, who was put in charge of the missing persons enquiry began it. Given the job of taking a statement from Haigh as a matter of routine, she took an instant dislike to him, observing that he was quite out of place among the residents of a hotel who were mainly elderly and wealthy. She also discovered from the hotel manageress that he had not been paying his bill too promptly of late, and was obviously in some state of financial embarrassment.

She sent a personal memo to the head of Chelsea CID, Detective Chief Inspector Shelley Symes. He, acting with sound instincts, checked the name John George Haigh against the criminals records file at Scotland Yard and, to his astonishment, out tumbled a long list of fraud convictions dated 1934, 1937 and 1943. That was all Symes needed to set out on a major enquiry. And he pursued it relentlessly.

Symes and a senior colleague, Detective Inspector Albert Webb, interviewed Haigh twice in four days at a private office inside the hotel. He answered all their questions coolly and confidently, once more playing the part of a friend wanting only to be helpful.

Openly he admitted that he had had an appointment with Olive on the day she disappeared. They were going to see a business partner who ran a small light-engineering firm in Crawley called Hurstlea Products and had agreed to meet outside the Army and Navy Stores in Victoria at 2.30 p.m. "I waited until nearly half-past three, and as she did not arrive I went on alone to Crawley", he told the detectives.

He was very plausible, but the detectives' suspicions remained. They set about checking his story.

The Sussex police were alerted to the case of the missing hotel guest on the morning of Tuesday, February 22, when Symes called the head of Horsham CID, Detective Sergeant Patrick Heslin and asked him to investigate Haigh's activities in Crawley and, in particular, to have a look at the premises of Hurstlea Products in West Street.

The detectives interviewed Edward Jones, owner of Hurstlea, and he confirmed that his partner John Haigh had been due to call on the Friday with someone who wanted to discuss making artificial fingernails. But the visitor had not turned up. No-one mentioned the little workshop in Leopold Road, just a mile away.

There was every prospect that this would end up being just another unsolved missing persons enquiry, as another four days slipped by. However, a moment of inspiration on the part of the Horsham CID chief Heslin suddenly turned the tide. With his Metropolitan Police colleague back in London, Heslin decided to forgo the chance of a Saturday off and, in the company of uniformed sergeant Appy Appleton, he set off on an impromptu tour of questioning around the small community of Crawley.

They talked again with Edward Jones at West Street and in a casual conversation he let drop that Hurstlea had been started four years previously in a small building at Giles Yard in Leopold Road. That building was still used for storage purposes, but "sometimes John borrowed it for his private work."

At 11.45 a.m. the detective was breaking the lock on the door with a metal bar. Inside he discovered a remarkable collection of implements and equipment, including three carboys of sulphuric acid, a stirrup pump, a gas mask, a large rubber apron, rubber gloves, rubber boots, a pad of cotton wool and some sheets of red cellophane paper. Although this was odd, it could still be explained as being compatible with work for some engineering requirement. But Haigh had made his first major blunder. He had decided that it would be safe to leave his precious leather hat-box and his personal leather briefcase in the workshop. Heslin found them both on a small table in the corner of the room.

From them he took documents of all types – passports, driving licences, ration books and diaries – many of them in the names of the McSwans and the Hendersons. Packed neatly at the bottom of the hat-box was the gun in its leather holster. From between the pages of a ration book there fluttered a receipt from a dry-cleaning shop, for a woman's fur.

Symes and Heslin went on the Sunday to the dry-cleaning shop at Reigate and there recovered Mrs Durand-Deacon's fur. On the Monday morning, a jeweller at Horsham rang the police to say he had purchased some rings and a necklace that had been listed in newspapers as belonging to a missing woman. And Arnold Burlin in Manchester was dialling 999 having just read in his paper that a Mr Haigh had been questioned in connection with a missing woman.

The police needed no more. Haigh was arrested at 4.15 p.m. on the same day, as he was about to step into his car outside the Onslow Court Hotel. During the evening he faced a barrage of new questions inside the interview room at Chelsea police station.

At first he tried to bluff, but when the police produced the gems and the fur he realized that the game was up. During a brief interlude in the questioning, he found himself alone with Detective Inspector Webb, and there is no doubt that in those few minutes he considered his predicament and decided on how he might save himself from the gallows. "Tell me, frankly, what are the chances of anyone being released from Broadmoor?" he asked Webb. "I cannot discuss that sort of thing with you," replied the astonished detective. Haigh continued: "Well, if I told you the truth you would not believe me; it sounds too fantastic for belief. Mrs Durand-Deacon no longer exists. She has disappeared completely and no trace can ever be found again. I have destroyed her with acid. You will find the sludge which remains at Leopold Road. Every trace has gone. How can you prove murder if there is no body?"

The startled Webb hurriedly recalled Symes to the room along with the head of Chelsea police, Superintendent Tom Barrett. The three policemen spent the next six hours listening to one of the most remarkable confessions ever heard in a police station as quietly and calmly Haigh revealed for the first time all his murdering exploits since 1944.

Almost proudly, he told of his Gloucester Road basement and the McSwans. Of the Crawley workshop and the Hendersons. And the callous killing of Olive Durand-Deacon only ten days previously. Instead of a confession to one murder, suddenly they had six. And there was more to come.

With a serious expression, the little man sitting in the chair explained that his motive for this carnage had been his desire to drink blood.

Describing the killing of Mrs Durand-Deacon, he went on: "Having taken her into the store-room at Leopold Road I shot her in the back of the head while she was examining some paper for use as fingernails. I then went out to the car and fetched in a drinking glass and made an incision, I think with a penknife, in the side of her throat, and collected a glass of blood, which I then drank."

There was an air of unreality, almost fantasy, inside the police station when the long statement was finally signed at 2.00 a.m.

During the next few weeks a Scotland Yard team led by a senior Flying Squad officer, Chief Detective Inspector Guy Mahon, set out to verify Haigh's statements. Their work showed conclusively that virtually everything said by John George Haigh was the truth.

There was one exception. They could not prove that he had drunk his victim's blood. For that they only had his word, although, intriguingly, Mahon did recover a penknife from the glove compartment of Haigh's car and a forensic scientist found traces of human blood on it. Fleet Street headlines, though, dubbed Haigh The Vampire and the name stuck. But most of the lawyers and psychiatrists who were drawn into the case came to the conclusion that Haigh had invented his lust for blood simply so that he could demonstrate to a court his insanity, and thus escape the noose.

There were some dramatic scenes outside Horsham Magistrates Court when they charged him with murder in the small Sussex town on Wednesday, March 2, and even more remarkable events took place at Crawley when the famous pathologist Dr. Keith Simpson was called in by police to examine the yard at Leopold Road.

Haigh contended that the police would find nothing because the acid had done its job so well. But he had not reckoned with the progress of forensic science. Within minutes of arriving at the yard, Simpson was down on his hands and knees foraging through soil where the prisoner had said that he had spilled out the contents of his gruesome drums.

From rubble and pebbles just below a clump of elderberry bushes he picked up what might have been a small rounded stone about the size of a cherry. "I think that's a gallstone!" he declared to the amazed Symes and Mahon who stood over him. "That looks like another."

Simpson had 475 pounds of soil from the yard moved in boxes to the Scotland Yard laboratories in London. There a team of scientists recovered 28 pounds of body fat, dozens of human bone fragments, and a set of perfectly preserved false dentures which were unaffected by their immersion in acid. A dentist was able to say conclusively that they had been made for Mrs Durand-Deacon.

These remnants were to demonstrate to Haigh that his long held theory of perfect murder was in ruins. However, the scientists did reveal that all fragments – including the acrylic resin teeth – would have eventually vanished had they been left in the acid-logged soil. Had Haigh kept quiet about his methods, he might just have got away with it.

The trial at Lewes Assizes in July, 1949, received a tremendous build-up from the press. The Attorney General, Sir Hartley Shawcross, led for the prosecution and an equally prominent politician and former Attorney General, David Maxwell Fyfe, was briefed for the defence. In fact, the whole issue was wrapped up quickly, in under two days.

The case for the Crown was devastatingly thorough. Haigh's only hope was to show that he was insane when he committed the crimes and Fyfe put all his resources into that single objective. There was no cross-examination of the 33 prosecution witnesses and the defendant was not called into the witness box.

Everything hinged on the testimony of one vital defence witness, Dr Henry Yellowlees, an eminent Harley Street psychiatrist, in whose opinion John Haigh was suffering from a rare form of pure paranoia and was, therefore, not responsible for his actions.

The doctor sounded very convincing at first, but he wilted under cross-examination by Shawcross. First he was forced to admit that he had seen Haigh in his cell only three times rather than the five he had claimed. Then he got in an awful tangle when Shawcross suggested that his conclusion as to Haigh's mental state had been based entirely on Haigh's own words, and that "the prisoner is a person on whose word it would be utterly unsafe to rely".

The question of insanity hinged on whether the defendant knew what he was doing was wrong. Shawcross and Yellowlees parried over the issue at length but it was obvious that the lawyer had the doctor on the run and he eventually cornered him in a final devastating exchange.

Shawcross: "I am not asking you whether the man decided in obedience to a higher power to do what he realised was wrong. I am asking you to look at the facts and tell the jury whether there is any doubt that he must have known that according to English law he was preparing to do and subsequently had done something which was wrong?"

Yellowlees: "I will say 'yes' to that if you say 'punishable by law' instead of 'wrong'."

Shawcross: "Punishable by law and, therefore, wrong by the law of this country?"

Yellowlees: "Yes, I think he knew that."

In that moment the case for the defence collapsed and John Haigh's bid to pull off the biggest con of his life – to pose as a blood-drinking maniac – had failed.

The jury took only 17 minutes to find him guilty of murder and the judge, 82-year-old Travers Humphreys, donned the black cap to pronounce the death sentence.

Haigh showed no emotion and spent his last days in the death cell at Wandsworth apparently quite content with his lot, not disputing the verdict or the work of the law.

Before he was executed on August 10, a few days after his 40th birthday, he made several final requests, the most extraordinary of which was for his green hopsack suit to be donated to Madame Tussaud's waxworks museum in London, where they were constructing a wax figure of him for the Chamber of Horrors.

There it remains today.

6
THE DOCTOR AND THE
ROLLS ROYCE
The Acquisitive Career of Dr Bodkin Adams

The tongues had been wagging in Eastbourne for more than twenty years. Why did quite so many patients leave gifts in their wills to one ordinary doctor? How could he afford to run four cars, including a Rolls Royce? Did he have a special power of persuasion over people?

Much of the gossip was simple chatter over the garden fence by people with nothing better to do. Others closer to the source talked more discreetly, in hushed whispers. A few were blatantly malicious.

At the height of this speculation, which ran rife in the famous Sussex seaside resort through the 1950s, there were a few people prepared to go even further – to allege that the doctor concerned was subjecting his patients to "hypnotic" drugs so that he could more easily induce them to part with their fortunes. Even worse, that he was precipitating their deaths once the will was signed, or at least allowing them to die without proper medical treatment. There was a local joke that when the doctor set out on his round of elderly patients he always took along a blank will form and a bottle of morphia.

The stories persisted for many years, until finally they swept the portly, bespectacled Dr John Bodkin Adams into the dock at the Old Bailey and to within a hair's-breadth of the gallows.

This rumour-mongering did not seem much to bother Dr Adams in the early days. He did not let it disturb his comfortable bachelor life and he went on, apparently oblivious, with his rounds as a G.P. He was never, though, content to be simply the family doctor. He wanted to be the family lawyer too. For when any chance presented it, he was prepared to offer an aging patient advice on how to make out a will. As a result, numerous elderly ladies appointed him their sole executor, he was regularly named as a minor beneficiary in their wills, and he often picked up the rich pickings that can accrue from the position of residuary legatee.

Even if well-intentioned, this was, by any standards, outrageous and indefensible professional behaviour. The real lawyers were not amused. Other doctors were appalled. Many shunned him, and the gossip ran riot.

The fact that it took so long to bring the genial Dr Adams to book was because his patients thought so much of him. Numerous residents of Eastbourne found him to be a paternal figure with qualities of kindness and understanding and were quite ready to vouch for his sympathetic treatment and good Christian manners.

Indeed when he had applied for his first medical job in the town during 1922 he had been drawn to the vacancy for "a Christian young doctor-assistant with a view to partnership" through an evangelical newspaper. And his qualifications were well suited to the three partners, Snowball, Harris and Barkworth, who took him in. Adams himself told a detective later that it was "all God's guidance and leading that had brought me to Eastbourne".

He was unusual in several respects. In later life he cut a portly figure with prominent spectacles on his rounded face that gave him a Dickensian air. Being a confirmed bachelor perhaps set him apart from the regular social scene and some may have viewed him as a singular and perhaps lonely figure. But in fact he gained much satisfaction from his work and poured his remaining time into a variety of hobbies which included photography, clay-pigeon shooting and motor cars.

Being brought up in a fairly strict Methodist environment, he lived to a code which included abstinence from alcohol. He always supported the local church, being a teacher at Sunday school when he could, and competently took the chair of the management committee at the Eastbourne Y.M.C.A.

Honest, clean-living ways were instilled into him from childhood in the Northern Ireland community of Randalstown where he was born on January 21,

1899, the son of a respected jeweller and Protestant J.P. His subsequent lifelong bachelorhood may be explained by the two tragedies he suffered while still only a teenager, the death of his father when 15 and the loss of his only brother three years later.

His mother was a strong church woman and ardent temperance worker, however the losses no doubt left her somewhat reliant on John and she came to live with her son in his large Eastbourne house until her death in 1943.

After first studying at Coleraine, Adams worked hard on his medical studies at Queen's University in Belfast, where he obtained a degree in medicine and surgery and was registered as a medical practitioner in 1921, at the age of 22.

His first post was as ophthalmic house surgeon and casualty officer at the Royal Infirmary in Bristol, but in 1922 he was lured to Eastbourne by the prospect of a partnership which he subsequently obtained, eventually becoming the senior in a lucrative four man practice. Queens awarded him his doctorate in 1926 and he went on to become a skilled anaesthetist, gaining a diploma in that subject during 1941 and the appointment of anaesthetist to the Eastbourne Hospital Group.

This successful career in Sussex brought him good financial rewards from a National Health panel of 800 patients plus a number of wealthy and influential private patients. By the year 1930 he was doing well enough to purchase a substantial 18-room house known as Kent Lodge, situated in the centre of Eastbourne at Trinity Trees, where he ran his own surgery and enjoyed the considerable comfort of a housekeeper, a receptionist, a secretary and a permanent chauffeur to drive him and care for his precious collection of cars, which included two MG Magnettes, a Morris Minor and a Rolls Royce.

Most of the Sussex seaside towns have a reputation for providing retirement havens and Eastbourne was top of that league; it was therefore inevitable that a large proportion of his clientele were ageing and that many had sufficient funds to make their final days by the sea comfortable. Helpfully situated near to Kent Lodge was the Esperance Nursing Home, one of several in the resort which specialized in caring for the elderly and where the doctor was a regular, and welcome, caller. He had the knack of winning the confidence of the old people entrusted to his care.

Not surprisingly, grateful patients occasionally left him small legacies. After all, it was not an uncommon practice to reward faithful servants in this way. An elderly widow might have only few next of kin, and her G.P. was often the person she most confided in. Adams was not the first G.P. to be rewarded in this

Kent Lodge, the Eastbourne home and surgery of Dr Bodkin Adams, as it looks today.

manner, but he did seem to get rather more of these presents than the average doctor.

It is perhaps impossible now to trace the precise moment when it all started, but Adams's acquisitive tendencies were already being displayed in 1935, when he was only 36. The elderly and very ill Mrs Matilda Whitton made him executor of her will and on her death he received £3,000, which in those times was a small fortune. Another £500 went to his cousin Sarah Henry and £100 to his mother. Mrs Whitton's relatives were not happy, and they ensured that the gossips of Eastbourne had plenty to chew over when they challenged the will in the High Court. The court did quash the £100 bequest to Adams's mother, but ruled the remainder in perfect order.

Over the next 22 years he received a constant flow of gifts from the dead. Police estimates identified 14 major windfalls, totalling £21,600, between 1944 and 1955. Somerset House records later revealed that during a period of some 35 years, between his beginning practice in 1922 and the momentous year of 1957, he benefitted from 132 wills in all. Many of the bequests were quite small and they often came in the form of jewellery, furniture and sums of cash. However, once in a while the figures were very substantial indeed, including one of £5,000 in 1946 and £5,200 out of an estate of £7,000 in 1954.

In the early days the doctor may have been merely accepting graciously whatever came along, but there seems to have come a time when he was actively canvassing for legacies in a really unacceptable way. This wholly unprofessional activity was certainly at its height during 1948 and 1950, when the now wealthy Adams was treating the very rich Mrs Edith Morrell.

At the age of 79, Mrs. Morrell had suffered a stroke in Cheshire and was admitted to hospital with her left side paralysed. In the summer of 1948 she was moved by ambulance to an Eastbourne nursing home, where Dr Adams took her under his care, supervising her treatment for the next two years and four months.

The bedridden lady settled to stay at Marden Ash, situated in Beachy Head Road, where she required day and night attendance by nurses and where Dr Adams kept her in a "comfortable" condition with doses of morphia and heroin.

A senior shareholder in the White Star Shipping Company, Mrs Morrell had a very substantial estate, amounting to £157,000, which clearly occupied her mind for much of the time she spent in Eastbourne. She appointed a local solicitor, Hubert Sogno, to take care of her affairs and often consulted him about her will, which she changed substantially on no less than six occasions.

On April 28, 1949, Adams telephoned Sogno urging him to visit the nursing home to see Mrs Morrell because she was "extremely anxious" about the contents of her will and wanted to change it on that very day. Sogno did as he was bid. He drew up a new will under which the bulk of Mrs Morrell's estate went to her son, but which left to the doctor an oak chest containing a valuable silver canteen of cutlery.

That event might have passed into obscurity. However, one year later, on March 8, 1950, Adams called at Sogno's office with a more dramatic demand: Mrs. Morrell had promised him her Rolls Royce and had forgotten to put this in her will. Although he admitted that she was "very ill", her mind was perfectly clear and he had no doubt that she was in a fit condition to make a codicil – immediately.

This time the solicitor was more cautious – he wanted a consultation with members of the family first. But Mrs Morrell's son was obviously sympathetic to his mother's wishes and so a codicil was added to her will on July 19 which left Adams her house and personal chattels if her son died before her. This was superseded, though, when a new, and final, will was drawn up on August 24 leaving the bulk of the estate to her son. There were smaller bequests – £1,000 to her chauffeur, £500 (and all the dahlias) to a gardener, £300 to a nurse and sums ranging from one pound to a thousand to six charities. To Dr Adams, Mrs

Morrell left silver valued at £275 and – but only if her son predeceased her – her Rolls Royce and an Elizabethan cupboard.

Mrs Morrell's health was deteriorating and she was given only weeks to live when in the September Dr Adams decided to take a holiday in Scotland. Mrs Morrell had become totally dependant on her doctor's presence and his absence angered her so much that she sent for her solicitor yet again to draw up a new codicil cutting the doctor out of her will completely. When Adams made a dramatic return to speak with her in the middle of his holiday, she tore up the codicil to signal that he was back in favour. But the mere act of tearing up the codicil did not nullify it – a new document, properly drawn up and properly authorised, was necessary to do that. So, ironically, when Mrs Morrell died at 2.00 a.m. on November 13, 1950, she had not legally re-instated Adams and he was left nothing.

But her son carried out what he knew to have been his mother's intentions. He saw to it that Dr Adams got his chest of silver and had the family chauffeur personally deliver the 1938 Rolls Royce to the doctor at his Kent Lodge home.

There the matter rested. The family had been content with the treatment Mrs Morrell had received. They carried out her wishes and scattered her ashes in the English Channel. The nurses who had eased her through the final months went on to other duties. The lawyers did their job settling the terms of the will. Dr Adams went off happily at the wheel of a Rolls.

No-one expressed even the slightest suspicion about the cause of death. No-one criticized the doctor for his high degree of interest in the will. If any questions were asked they were certainly not of an official nature, merely comments that joined the usual whispers and rumours.

Most surprisingly of all perhaps, no-one noticed a peculiarity on the cremation certificate that had been completed by Dr Adams. To the question asking if the signatory had any pecuniary interest in the deceased's estate, he had written: "Not as far as I am aware". Bearing in mind his extraordinary interest in Mrs Morrell's affairs and the gifts that were coming his way, this was at best very naive and at worst downright dishonest. The words were to haunt him years later.

More legacies came his way, but during the five years that followed Mrs Morrell's death, he committed no indiscretion serious enough to bring him to the notice of officialdom. Then, in 1956, came the affair that was to lead him straight into the arms of the law and the courts.

At the heart of it was another of his patients, Mrs Gertrude "Bobby" Tomlinson, a woman who came to have more than one reason to rely heavily on the help of her doctor. She was not yet 50, much younger than many of his other patients. She became his patient after the death of her first husband. Encouraged by Adams, she had gone on a long cruise with another patient of his, a wealthy widower, in his sixties, named Jack Hullett. The relationship had proved so successful that, on their return, they announced their engagement and later wed.

For the new Mrs Hullett there was an exciting new lease of life. A Lloyd's underwriter, her husband had plenty of money and together they shared a magnificent home at the foot of Beachy Head called Holywell Mount in Dukes Drive. On Jack's 70th birthday they entertained a hundred guests at the Savoy Hotel in London and they travelled extensively to Australia, New Zealand and America. But, sadly, there was a second tragedy in store for Gertrude Hullett. After having a major stomach operation in 1955 at the Esperance nursing home, Mr Hullett was taken ill at Holywell Mount in the early hours of March 14, 1956, and died in his sleep, apparently from cerebral haemorrhage and coronary thrombosis.

The bulk of his £94,644 estate passed to his widow, but there was £500 for Dr Adams. Once more, when authorizing the cremation certificate, the doctor denied that he stood to gain from the deceased's estate.

Mrs Hullett never recovered from the loss of her second husband; she slipped into a suicidal depression. Adams prescribed sodium barbiturate to help her sleep at night, but she was inconsolable. In July 1956, as though to wind up her affairs on earth, she made a final will. Her next of kin was to inherit her substantial estate, valued at £142,000, but there were gifts for various friends, including another Rolls Royce for Dr Adams.

Mrs Hullett knew that her late husband had also intended to buy a car as a present for Adams but had not mentioned that in his will. So on July 17 she simply wrote out a cheque for £1,000 made payable to the doctor in order to settle her mind on that subject. Adams took it to his bank on the 18th and requested special clearance so that there would be no delay getting it into his account.

On the morning of July 20 Mrs Hullett failed to waken from a deep sleep. At first the maid thought Mrs Hullett was simply sleeping late and it was not until later in the day that it was realized that she was seriously ill. Dr Adams and one of his partners, Dr Harris, consulted on her condition at 5.00 p.m.

Remarkably, Adams ruled out the possibility that she had taken an overdose of sleeping tablets because he believed that she had access to only two a day, those

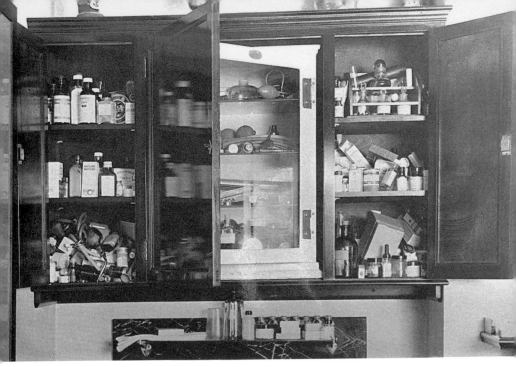

Dr Adams' medicine cabinet.

The surgery at Kent Lodge.

he had prescribed. He argued with Harris against moving her to hospital, because he claimed that "would be against her express wishes".

He did, however, search Mrs Hullett's bedroom for empty bottles or cartons and found none. He arranged for a night nurse to come in and he called on consultant pathologist Dr Arthur Shera to carry out some urgent blood and urine tests. And he later admitted that he obtained a supply of megimide, an antidote to barbiturates, "in view of the remote possibility of barbiturate poisoning".

Then, on the Sunday, came the most extraordinary action of all. With his patient in the third day of a coma, he rang the Eastbourne coroner to enquire about the possibility of a private post-mortem. The coroner, not amused, advised him to go through the proper procedures at the proper time.

Mrs Hullett died at 7.23 a.m. on Monday. Neither Adams nor Harris was confident enough to sign a death certificate. Instead, Adams wrote a most unusual letter, which was signed also by Dr Harris, to the coroner. In it he concluded: "In my and Dr Harris's opinion death was due to a cerebral lesion, probably involving the pons with secondary complications in the lungs. Because of the pathologist's findings being inconclusive, and cremation requested, we are reporting the facts fully to you – as we do not feel in a position to issue a death certificate". The final 13 words were added in pen by Harris.

The post-mortem revealed that cause of death had been a huge dose of barbiturates, totalling 115 grams, the equivalent of 20 tablets – 10 times higher than Mrs Hullett's prescribed daily dose.

The Eastbourne coroner, Dr Sommerville, had heard some of the talk about Dr Adams. He informed the Chief Constable of Sussex about Mrs Hullett's death. The Chief Constable, as was customary in those days when very serious crime was suspected, called in Scotland Yard.

When the adjourned inquest resumed on August 21 the whole of Eastbourne was buzzing with eager anticipation. The press benches were packed with reporters from newspapers across the whole of Britain. And sitting quietly near them was another observer, Detective Superintendent Herbert Hannam of the Metropolitan Police – Hannam of the Yard – a detective whose smart suits and occasional cigar had earned him the nickname of "the Count".

There was no talk of murder at the inquest, but there were some very pointed criticisms of the actions that had been taken prior to Mrs Hullett's death, and some tough questioning for the doctor to face.

Coroner: "Did you try your best for her at the very end?"

Adams: "I honestly did what I thought was the best for her in every way."

Coroner: "Did you clear away the tablets her husband had?"

Adams: "Frankly and honestly it didn't occur to me. I thought I had tied it up so well and it didn't occur to me."

The doctor had to admit that his patient might have concealed old sleeping tablets originally prescribed for her late husband and, even more significantly, he admitted giving her 36 tablets to last her over the period while he was on holiday.

The coroner in his summing up did not directly censure Adams, but he spoke of "a considerable quantity of barbiturate poison" being involved and asked: "Did she take these tablets, or were they given to her? And was there any negligence?". He continued:

You may consider it extraordinary that the doctor, knowing the past history of the patient, did not at once suspect barbiturate poisoning. If he had suspected barbiturate poisoning possibly the circumstances might have been otherwise.

There you have treatment that you may consider was not that form of treatment that a reasonable person should expect from a reasonable doctor. But on the other hand if the doctor was convinced in his own mind that there was no question of barbiturate poisoning then the treatment was quite normal for a cerebral catastrophe.

It is not enough to divert one degree of negligence into a more serious degree of negligence by error of judgement or carelessness in any degree. In considering criminal negligence one must know and believe and have proof that the death of the deceased is the direct cause of the doctor's negligence.

In this case you will no doubt come to the conclusion that this is not the case. If there has been an extraordinary element of careless treatment, in so far as the doctor knew the history of the patient and then did not disclose it, that is not criminal negligence.

The jury had already learned of Mrs Hullett's depression after the death of her husband and had been told how she had settled her affairs in her will. They concluded that she had taken the tablets herself "of her own free will", and they returned a verdict of suicide.

Adams was, for the moment anyway, off the hook.

But if the jurors of Eastbourne were satisfied, the Scotland Yard man sitting quietly in court certainly was not. He suspected wrong doing on a spectacular scale and he began a painstaking enquiry into the affairs of Dr John Bodkin Adams.

The investigation looked back over the past ten years, covering every patient who had left the doctor money. During nearly four months of frenzied police activity throughout Eastbourne and beyond, detectives interviewed nurses, relatives, friends, lawyers, chemists, undertakers, doctors and – crucially – experts on the use and effects of drugs.

Every move the police made was followed by the national press, in which the speculation at times ran riot. At one time it was suggested that Scotland Yard was investigating "the most sensational episode in British criminal history" and that 25 names would emerge as likely victims of a mass poisoner.

Hannam never did get that far, but he quite quickly uncovered a string of less serious offences. Dr. Adams would have to answer charges on them all.

From prescription forms, wills and death certificates, the Yard team soon learned of the propensity for bending rules that marked the career of Dr Adams. There were, most seriously, his false entries on cremation certificates – four in all, relating to Edith Morrell, Amy Ware, James Downs and Alfred Hullett. And there were minor problems with eight prescriptions, including two for a pair of elastic stockings for Dorothy Crisford and an elastic knee support for Beryl Galloway.

Hannam was not really an outrageously unorthodox copper, but he could not resist the chance to chat with the enigmatic doctor and during the evening of October 1 he "chanced" to be walking past the garages at Kent Lodge when Adams was putting his car away. There in the semi-darkness the two men had a most unusual conversation.

Their talk centred on Mrs Morrell and, in particular, on the cremation certificate. According to Hannam's notes, Adams declared: "Oh, that was not done wickedly. God knows it wasn't. We always want cremations to go off smoothly for the dear relatives. If I had said I knew I was getting money under the will they might get suspicious and I like cremations and burials to go off smoothly. There was nothing suspicious really. It was not deceitful."

They met again some seven weeks later, on Saturday, November 24. But this time it was official. In the company of Detective Sergeant Hewitt from the Yard and Detective Inspector Pugh of Eastbourne, Hannam formally arrested Dr Adams on 13 charges of forgery and false entries, and produced a warrant to search the surgery.

"What a shock. I am just going out to the Y.M.C.A.", declared the doctor.

Hannam found Adams's surgery to be in an "untidy" state; many medicine bottles were lying higgledy-piggledy on top of each other. In a medicine cupboard he discovered slabs of chocolate, packets of sugar, pieces of sticky margarine and butter – and a bottle with Mrs Hullett's name on it containing 22 tablets. Adams could not produce a register of dangerous drugs as required, and at one stage he was spotted slipping a couple of bottles of morphine from a shelf into his pockets. Three new charges to add to the thirteen already issued.

Before leaving the surgery at the end of the two-hour search, Hannam produced a statement he had taken from Eastbourne chemist H.R. Browne setting out all the prescriptions made out for Mrs Morrell.

"There are a lot of dangerous drugs here", declared the detective. "Who administered them?"

Adams: "I did, nearly all. Perhaps the nurses gave some, but mostly me."

Hannam: "Were there any of them left when she died?"

Adams: "No, none. All was given to the patient. Poor soul, she was in terrible agony."

Eastbourne magistrates gave the doctor bail of £1,000 when he faced the 13 minor charges on the Monday morning of November 26. The law had him in a corner now, but what of murder? Here was something much more difficult to identify.

Adams himself was intrigued and asked to see Hannam at the police station on the same day to learn what further enquiries were proceeding. Hannan told him bluntly: "I am still enquiring into the death of some of your rich patients," naming Mrs Morrell as one of them.

Adams replied: "Easing the passing of a dying patient is not all that wicked. She wanted to die. That cannot be murder. It is impossible to accuse a doctor."

But it *was* possible to accuse a doctor. Hannam found a startling number of relatives, and nurses too, who were critical of the treatment Adams had given and suspicious of the circumstances in which loved ones had died. There was talk of "persuasion" to alter wills during private bedside meetings, of an "indifferent" attitude in the final days and even of "huge doses" of morphine administered by hypodermic syringe hours before death.

Hannam's investigations had looked into 124 deaths that Adams had attended in ten years. From then Hannam drew up a short list of names on which he proposed to concentrate – they included Edith Morrell, Alfred Hullett, Gertrude Hullett, Julia Bradnum, Clara Neil-Miller, Amy Ware and James Downs.

In the last will and testament of 88-year-old James Priestly Downs, a former bank manager, the dispositions were all neatly typed out on a sheet of parchment – except for a late addition, in ink, that read "to Dr. John Bodkin Adams of 6, Trinity Trees, one thousand pounds". Amy Constance Ware, a resident of the Edgehill nursing home, had originally decided to leave the doctor £100 from her £8,993 estate, but just before her death in 1950 she increased that to £1,000. Adams signed the cremation certificates in both cases. And on both he had declared that he was not, "to my knowledge", a beneficiary of the estate.

Still near the top of the list for investigation were the Hulletts. The barbiturate poisoning of 50-year-old Gertrude Hullett remained of considerable significance to the Yard, in spite of the suicide verdict by a jury. The death of her husband Alfred also seemed suspicious. A nurse had described his passing as "unusual". On the day before he died he had been in good spirits and had enjoyed a drink of lager at the Pilot pub. Dr Adams called to give him a "highly concentrated injection of morphia" during the evening and he died at 6.45 a.m. next morning.

However, it was in the case of Edith Morrell − a death now six years past − that Hannam and his team believed they had found what they required. Through the record of prescriptions kept by Browne's the chemist they learned that Adams had prescribed for her staggeringly high doses of morphia and heroin − hypnotic and narcotic drugs that, in the opinion of forensic pathologist Dr Francis Camps, would almost certainly have resulted in addiction. The maximum daily doses of these drugs were a quarter of a grain of heroin and half a grain of morphia. During the last six days of her life, Mrs. Morrell had been prescribed heroin and morphia in the following amounts: November 8, 16½ grs; November 9, 18¾ grs; November 10, 6¼ grs; November 11, 18¾ grs; November 12, 12½ grs. This amounted to 78¾ grains, against the recommended dosage of 4½ grains.

There was, though, a difference between prescribing a drug and actually giving it to a patient. But Adams himself had said "all was given to the patient". So, armed with these figures, and backed by a high-powered legal conference in London, attended by the Attorney General and the Director of Public Prosecutions, Hannam decided to charge Adams with murder.

Before any further moves were made on the minor charges, the Scotland Yard man returned to Kent Lodge on December 19, just before Christmas 1956, to confront Adams yet again.

"Murder", exclaimed the doctor, "can you prove it was murder?" Later he added: "I didn't think you could prove murder, she was dying in any event." As he left for the police station, he gripped the hand of his shaken receptionist and said to her: "I will see you in heaven". When he was formally charged with the murder of Edith Alice Morrell, he replied merely: "It is better to say nothing."

Hannam continued to look for evidence in the other cases he was interested in. Only two days after Adams had been charged, Hannam led a team of police diggers to Ocklynge Cemetery at Eastbourne where, at 7.00 a.m. on December

21, they exhumed the body of Julia Bradnum. Two hours later they moved to Langney Cemetery to retrieve the remains of Clara Neil-Miller. There to make an examination was the Dr Francis Camps, and watching him on behalf of the accused man was the equally famous pathologist Dr Keith Simpson.

A former Eastbourne guest-house owner, Mrs Bradnum, had died suddenly; she was 85 but she had been very active. To the surprise of her relatives and friends, she had appointed Adams as sole executor of her will. He had taken an "active part" in helping her to change her will and, with five others, shared the proceeds of her estate. Mrs Neil-Miller died at the age of 87 four months after she had made Adams her sole executor and named him as "residuary legatee absolutely". Her death made Adams the richer by £1,275.

Mrs Bradnum and Mrs Neil-Miller were among the few suspected victims who had not been cremated. The police confidently believed that they would find considerable evidence of large drug doses. In fact, nothing of the kind was found. Due to the lapse of time, no analysis of the drugs was possible. The two experts agreed on one thing: that one of the two had died from cerebral thrombosis, exactly what the doctor had certified.

These exhumations received national publicity, but their outcome did not. The police were doing Dr Adams no favours. Naturally, most readers thought the worst about the accused doctor. The preliminary magistrates hearing, which got underway a couple of weeks later on January 14, confirmed most people's certainty of his guilt. In those days there were no restrictions on the reporting of committal hearings before local magistrates, and the entire, damning prosecution case was blazed across the front pages of the nation. It was because of the damage that was so obviously done to the name of the defendant in this remarkable hearing that the law was subsequently altered, so that those going for trial today do not have the evidence from a lower court publicized.

The prejudice in this case was blatantly obvious. Not only did the Crown prosecutor Mr Melford Stevenson Q.C., give details of the charge alleging the murder of Mrs Morrell, he proceeded to read out equally devastating allegations that both Mr and Mrs Hullett had been murdered too. It made sensational reading and there was hardly a soul who did not now believe that Dr Adams was destined for the gallows.

Stevenson spelled out the prosecution case. Mrs Morrell had "died because she was poisoned by drugs, mainly heroin and morphine, which Dr Adams administered, or caused to be administered to her, a short time before her death."

As for 71-year-old Mr Hullett, Dr Adams had given him an injection of "a highly concentrated form of morphia" at 10.30 p.m. and by 6.45 a.m. he was dead. "Again, we say that greed for money was the motive, and that greed was too great to permit him to wait, and that is why he killed Mr Hullett when he did," went on Stevenson.

The death of Mrs Hullett some four months later had been established by a post-mortem as being caused by barbitone poisoning, "and she died in circumstances which the Crown says amount to murder by Dr Adams, whether she herself administered the fatal dose, or whether she did not," said the prosecutor.

"The same pattern repeats itself. A rich patient. Heavy drugging over a period of months ending up with a fatal dose. A patient obviously under the influence of the doctor. A patient under whose will Dr Adams benefited. You get the impatience, the same desire for money, evidenced by the special clearance of that cheque for £1,000...." The words were devastating.

There seemed no hope for Adams now. The gossips had been pursuing him for years. The Hullett inquest had cast doubts on his professionalism. The press had branded him the villain of the century. The Yard was pursuing him relentlessly. The exhumations were linked to him. The Crown had charged him with one murder, but accused him in open court of three. Little wonder that the *Daily Express* journalist Percy Hoskins could write: "In my many years as a crime reporter I had seldom seen a man so neatly trussed up and ready for the scaffold...."

There was, however, one man left in Britain who might save him, and that was Geoffrey Lawrence Q.C., appointed by the Medical Defence Union to defend the doctor when the case came for trial in number one court at the Old Bailey. It was to become one of the classic murder trials of the decade. The protagonists were the defender Geoffrey Lawrence and the prosecuting counsel, the Attorney General, Sir Reginald Manningham-Buller. Lord Justice Devlin presided.

The hearing was concerned only with the death of Mrs Morrell and the outcome depended on proving that Adams was responsible for administering to her lethal doses of morphine or heroin. There to support the Crown case were four nurses who had attended her – Nurse Randall, Sister Mason-Ellis, Nurse Stronach and Sister Bartlett – and two eminent medical men, Dr Arthur Douthwaite, a senior physician at Guys and a recognized expert on narcotic drugs, and Dr Michael Ashby, a Harley Street neurologist and consultant to six London hospitals.

Manningham-Buller began confidently:

The nurses will tell you that during her last days she was comatose or semi-conscious. And that brings us back to the question – why did the doctor prescribe such quantities, such fatal quantities, for which there is no medical justification?

The submission of the Crown is that he did so because he had decided that the time had come for her to die ....

And later:

You will hear that the maximum quantity of heroin which should be prescribed in a period of 24 hours is a quarter of a grain. Yet no less than eight grains were prescribed by the doctor on a single day. The maximum dose of morphia is half a grain. There were ten grains prescribed on the eighth of November, twelve on the ninth and eighteen on the 11th. The prosecution will call medical authority who will tell you that in their view Mrs Morrell could not possibly have survived the administration of these drugs prescribed in her last five days.

The court settled down to listen to the nurses, first Stronach who was gently and efficiently persuaded by junior Crown counsel Melford Stevenson to recall her memory of Mrs Morrell's treatment and condition in the last days of her life. Her evidence seemed fatal for Adams. But, unknown to all but a few in the enthraled court room, the defence team was relishing the situation. Among the papers on the desk in front of Geoffrey Lawrence was a small pile of eight notebooks. They had been in the possession of Dr Adams for five years, brought to Kent Lodge by the Morrell family chauffeur after her death, and "lost" among hundreds of other papers and mementoes that the doctor had never had the heart to destroy. They had been unearthed through the diligence of family solicitor M.V. James, who had searched rooms at Kent Lodge for anything that might assist his client facing a charge of murder. The books were tucked into the back of a filing-cabinet drawer, wrapped in a brown-paper parcel, unopened. And they contained a complete record of Mrs Morrell's daily treatment – a record made by the nurses themselves.

When Lawrence cross-examined Nurse Stronach he got her to agree that all experienced nurses recorded each injection they gave; everything of importance was written down; such writings would be accurate because they would be written on the day that they happened; and, of course, such a record would be much more accurate than the memory of six years later. Then, dramatically, he produced the notebooks. And with them he changed the entire course of the trial.

Devastatingly for the nurse he demonstrated that her memory of 1950 was poor, to say the least. Line by line, day by day, he produced discrepancies and inconsistencies until her credibility as a witness simply crumbled.

This was typical of the many exchanges:

Lawrence: "Let us see what you put down for the day only one month before she died. The entry for 4 p.m. says 'patient became restless and picking at bedclothes' and this in your writing 'Hypo injection Omnopon two thirds given at 4.40 p.m. You gave it..."

Stronach: "Yes".

Lawrence: "Do not think I am blaming you or criticising you, but you told me earlier this morning that you never had given Mrs Morrell any injection except morphia."

Stronach: "I believed that was true".

Lawrence: "What this entry shows is that your memory was playing you a trick, does it not?"

Stronach: "Apparently so."

Lawrence: "Obviously so."

The original picture of the doctor calling regularly, excluding nurses from the room and pumping massive doses into a comatose woman was fading rapidly. Indeed, the notebooks demonstrated that Mrs Morrell never lapsed into coma and was having regular food up to the end. Throughout the remainder of the evidence from the nurses, Manningham-Buller was forced to tread a very wary path, knowing now that the words of his star witnesses might be compromised at any time by these intimidating notebooks.

As a final touch, Lawrence pointed out that one of the nurses had herself received a gift of £50 from Mrs Morrell's son in appreciation of her care.

Round one had certainly gone to the defence, but there were still the medical experts to come – in particular the distinguished and handsome Dr Arthur Douthwaite, the Crown's star witness.

Manningham-Buller: "Is there any justification or legitimate ground in your view for administering heroin and morphia together?"

Douthwaite: "No".

Manningham-Buller: "What can be the medical object of giving a routine injection of morphia and heroin?"

Douthwaite: "There isn't one".

Manningham-Buller: "What conclusions do you draw from the dosage administered in the last days, what conclusions do you draw as to the intentions

Dr John Bodkin Adams. *(Photo: Press Association)*

A prescription signed by Dr Adams and fulfilled by G.A. Harmer & Son, Chemist.

with which that dosage must have been prescribed?"

Douthwaite: "The only conclusion I can come to is that the intention on November 8 was to terminate her life".

How could Lawrence possibly counter that? Once more he proved to be a master at his job. With another dramatic production of medical records, he showed that before her arrival in Eastbourne Mrs Morrell had been receiving daily injections of morphia under the supervision of two doctors in Cheshire. Adams was merely continuing that treatment. Surely Dr Douthwaite was not questioning the competence of those doctors as well?

Remarkably, Lawrence also got Douthwaite to admit that heroin could be useful in certain situations and that if a patient obviously had a short time to live – as had Mrs Morrell – it became pointless worrying about addiction to drugs. In other words, Dr Adams might simply have been doing his best as her G.P. to ease her pain and give her comfort in the last days.

The fencing between the lawyer and the medical expert was a classic courtroom confrontation that went on for many hours, but it was in that moment that many experienced Old Bailey observers felt that the tide had been turned.

The Crown's second medical witness, Dr Michael Ashby, merely reinforced the growing sense of relief that must have been flooding through the silent Dr Adams. He was unable to rule out the possibility that a patient of 81 with such a medical history had not simply died of natural causes.

The defence called their own medical expert, Dr John Harman, consulting physician at St Thomas's Hospital in London, who throughout a tough cross-examination by the Attorney General stoutly rejected Douthwaite's evidence and firmly expounded his own theory that neither morphine or heroin had caused the death.

Judge Devlin took the trial into its 17th day during a summing up that clearly pointed to a not guilty verdict, and that is what the jury brought in on April 9, 1957, after retiring for only 45 minutes.

Defeat for the Crown was total. It was well known that the prosecuting authorities already had a second indictment lined up against Adams if the first failed: that of the alleged murders of Mr and Mrs Hullett. But, while the courtroom was still taking in the significance of the verdict they had just heard, Sir Reginald Manningham-Buller was on his feet to declare that in view of all the circumstances there would be no further prosecutions.

Of course, that was not the end of the Adams affair. The repercussions were many and varied, including questions in the House of Commons on the role of the prosecution.

In the June of that year, Dr Adams resigned his N.H.S. post, knowing that he would have to plead guilty to the sixteen "minor" offences which brought him before Lewes Assizes in the July. Those misdemeanours cost him a £2,400 fine and when the General Medical Council met in the November he was, inevitably, struck off the register.

But from the brink of being marched off to the gallows, Dr John Bodkins Adams made a remarkable comeback. Four years later he was reinstated and resumed his practice at Kent Lodge in Eastbourne. Many of his old patients returned to him – there was no doubt that his patients genuinely liked him.

Many people felt that he was fortunate to have been let off so lightly. Others had defended him solidly throughout. Standing somewhere between these two attitudes was the judge who had presided over the Old Bailey trial, Patrick Devlin.

He believed that the verdict was correct on the evidence presented, but wrote, in his book *Easing the Passing*:

This does not mean that Dr Adams was not a murderer, only that he was not a monster. He might have murdered – it must be remembered that euthanasia is murder – either as a mercy-killer or perhaps just to finish off a troublesome patient who was dying anyway and for whom he could do no more.

The mercenary mercy-killer fits best the picture of him that I have in mind. Certainly he had one characteristic which is a good qualification for a killer of that sort, a disposition to think lightly of the law. The cases to which he confessed at Lewes Assizes show a reluctance to be bothered with it.

Devlin labelled him "an ignorant and incompetent" doctor and a "greedy" man. But his greed was that of a miser rather than of a big spender. He was acquisitive throughout his life, and, on his death in July, 1983, at the age of 84, he left an estate worth £402,970. At Kent Lodge his executors discovered many articles untouched and unused. Percy Hoskins has revealed that a £10,000 fee paid to him by the *Daily Express* for his story remained in an envelope unopened between 1957 and 1983.

The doctor just liked to keep things. A habit which, to all intents and purposes, extended his active life by a further 26 years. For without the nursing records that were left casually inside an unopened parcel at his Eastbourne surgery, the Old Bailey trial might have had a wholly different outcome.

Many doctors would have dumped them. Adams didn't. And they saved him from the hangman.

7
DEATH IN THE ARUN
The Killing of Jonathan Lewis, 1980

The whole of Europe was suffering from *Jeux Sans Frontières* disease. The fever had penetrated even to the sleepy Sussex towns of Littlehampton and Arundel, where, on the night of Wednesday July 23, 1980, a major international heat of Eurovision's famous "It's a Knockout" competition was being staged. A spectacular arena had been set up in the grounds of the Avisford Park Hotel at Walburton, a few miles from Arundel. Compères Eddie Waring and Stuart Hall were there in glittering fancy dress and a crowd of 8,000 watched teams of various nationalities competing in crazy games under the floodlights. The theme was magic, with giant toppers, wands, dice, playing cards and jokers dominating the colourful scene, every second being captured by TV cameras for an estimated audience of 600 million people across the world.

What none of those millions could know, of course, was that behind this facade of summer jollity a more sinister story was unfolding. A story of a love triangle, of clandestine meetings and a shocking death on the banks of the picturesque River Arun.

In the arena the games concluded with the defeat of the local Arun team, but nevertheless the show was hailed a great success all round, especially for Arun District Council, the sponsors, and notably for that local authority's information and liaison officer, Colin Wallace.

Since joining the council in 1976, Wallace had demonstrated a great dedication to his work and was recognized as a superb organizer. Some called him a perfectionist and a workaholic. Arun councillors had given him full responsibility for supervising their part in the running of this popular event along with a team which included his assistant, Jane Lewis, and tourism officers Ned Wayne and Tony Baker.

Everything went with military precision, and that was not surprising for the man with bright blue eyes and a gentle Irish brogue had come from a disciplined environment in his home country of Northern Ireland where he had been prominent in the Territorial Army at Randalstown, had helped train cadets and had undertaken numerous parachute drops in his role as a part-time soldier.

Military ways fascinated him. He had been a member of the Ulster Special Constabulary and attained the rank of captain while serving in the volunteer Ulster Defence Regiment. It was while with the Territorials that he was sent with 150 others on an important visit to New Zealand, where he participated in military exercises which included brief attachment to an SAS unit.

Wallace obtained qualifications at Queen's University in Belfast which led him to a responsible post in a hospital pathology laboratory, but it was army life that attracted him most and he grasped at the opportunity, when it came, to set out on a different career as a full-time public relations officer with the regular army based at Lisburn. In 1974, at the age of 29, he was appointed senior information officer. He seemed to be on the brink of an outstanding career with the British Army. Then suddenly – and mysteriously – he had given it all up.

His work had moved on from merely dealing with routine press releases to one that encompassed what some have described as "black propaganda", the feeding of disinformation to reliable sources in order to create havoc among the ranks of the enemy. The story is that this brought him into close contact with the security services and the little known world of "dirty tricks" first against the IRA and then in a shadowy plot allegedly designed to discredit leading politicians of the day.

Wallace has declared that he eventually recoiled against this work and moves were made to get rid of him. Shortly after he was moved to work in England, an enquiry took place into the passing of a sensitive military document by Wallace to *Times* journalist Robert Fisk. After a high-powered civil service hearing in London, he was dismissed but because of his previous good record was given the opportunity to step down graciously.

Bitterly he resigned the job he loved and for many months lived in Preston without work. When the post at Arun District Council in Littlehampton turned up in 1976 he took it gratefully as just the chance he needed to start again. He and his wife Eileen, and their large sheepdog, set up a comfortable home in a select suburb of Arundel.

As far as everyone in Sussex was concerned, the Wallaces were a big success and warmly accepted into the community. He quickly gained a wide circle of influential friends while Eileen's organizational skills won her the post of secretary to the Duke of Norfolk at Arundel Castle. The Duke was soon counted among their close associates.

Both attracted friends readily, and into their lives came 27-year-old Jane, Colin's assistant at the council information department, and her husband Jonathan Lewis, a 29-year-old antiques dealer with a shop in Brighton's famous Lanes. They were a handsome young couple who married in the summer of 1979 and lived together a few miles out of Arundel in the village of Angmering.

The Wallaces and the Lewises made a foursome – together they enjoyed the social scene that life in public relations can bring and Colin and Jonathan enjoyed regular games of squash together. But Colin and Jane, thrown together through their work on the *Jeux Sans Frontières* project, became closer still. They graduated to a more amorous liaison when they both accompanied the Arun team and a group of councillors to Charnock Richard in Lancashire for a British heat of the contest. In a hotel there 37-year-old Colin spoke of his love for Jane, ten years his junior, and they kissed and cuddled in his bedroom.

When the Arun organizers went to visit Switzerland to see how a Eurovision spectacular worked, Colin and Jane were with them once more and for one night shared a hotel room. During this trip they discussed their respective marriages and, according to Wallace, agreed that they did not want the affair to affect their spouses in any way.

Immediately after the Arundel contest had been completed they spent more time in each other's company, taking long walks together and enjoying a picnic lunch in Arundel Park. "At that time I responded to him more than I had previously and in doing so probably encouraged him a little more," Jane later revealed. However, it seems that they both accepted that the relationship could not continue, and talked about seeking jobs elsewhere in order to extricate themselves from the situation. Their short-lived affair, such as it was, was always one-sided. Jane was not in love with Colin. Their affair, both agree, never went as far as adultery.

Jane and Jonathan had never openly discussed the situation, but Jonathan may well have suspected that something was going on between Jane and Colin. However, at the end of July, 1980, there is evidence to show that Jane and Jonathan, having gone through a rough patch in their short marriage, were drawing closer together again. The mood between them on Sunday, August 3, was loving, and next day they were enthusiastically celebrating their first wedding anniversary with a dinner for two at Chichester and eagerly preparing for a holiday they were to start on the following Friday.

In that busy summer week, Colin had organized two celebration parties at the Avisford Park Hotel to thank those who had worked on the Eurovision contest. Jane and Jonathan missed the first because it coincided with their anniversary dinner, but were invited to the second on the following evening of Tuesday, August 5.

Jane had been conned into believing that she was merely going to another business meeting on council matters, and, after a hard day's work and an early evening game of squash with Eileen, must have been feeling a little weary at the prospect. In fact, she found herself walking straight into a surprise thank-you dinner party arranged by her boss. And, no doubt to her further astonishment, it was she who was given place of honour as the principal guest.

There to welcome her were a dozen others, mostly prominent people who had worked together organizing the highly successful event that had put the Arun valley on the international TV map – among them the Arundel police superintendent William Taylor, who had been responsible for traffic and arena safety.

It began so well and should have been yet another organizational triumph, so typical of the Wallace touch. In fact, it became a night of tragedy – a night that Jane is never likely to forget, and a night that changed irrevocably the course of Colin's career.

Jonathan was due to arrive at the hotel separately, coming straight from his work to take his place alongside his wife next to Colin and Eileen. But his place at the table remained empty.

At first Colin was able to allay the mild concern by revealing that Jonathan had telephoned him earlier indicating that he might be late because of another appointment. Jane ordered a meal for him, but it was never eaten. As the evening wore on without any further word, Jane's anxiety began to show. She knew that her husband would not have failed to contact her if for any reason he could not attend.

Telephone calls to their home at Ferndale Walk, Angmering, and to Jonathan's warehouse at Portslade brought no reply. As the subdued party broke up at about midnight, real fear began to take hold.

Another minor incident also marred the celebration. Wallace the host was suffering from a recurrence of a stomach disorder which meant he did not enjoy the meal and had to excuse himself from the gathering for a period of about forty minutes so that he could go back to his home in Dalloway Road, Arundel, to collect some tablets. At the time, his absence from the table went by without fuss, but later it was to occupy the keen attention of both the police and a jury.

Jane, now seriously concerned, with Colin and Eileen, went directly from the hotel to her home at Angmering. There she tried to find out what had happened to Jonathan, ringing friends, speaking to neighbours and contacting some of his associates in the antiques business. They rang hospitals and informed Jonathan's parents, Colonel and Mrs Sidney Lewis in Worthing, who were partners in the business.

Despite the late hour, an antique-dealer friend who lived in the village, John Muggeridge, drove with his wife to Church Road, Portslade, to check Jonathan's warehouse and then went on to Prince Albert Street in Brighton to look over his shop. Nothing was found. At 4.00 a.m. they called the police.

Only one fact emerged from these efforts – a next-door neighbour had seen Jonathan leaving the house on Tuesday evening in his distinctive orange Volvo estate at about 6.15 p.m. No-one had seen sight of him, or the car, since.

Jane already had one nagging theory. Her husband had many contacts in the antiques business. His own business was in the upper end of the market and his reputation was impeccable, but within the antiques trade there is an underworld element in which violence is not unknown. Jonathan had had some business disagreements and had warned his wife that, if anything should happen to him, to be wary of one particular gentleman. She recalled his words now. And her suspicions were shared by family friend John Muggeridge, who knew Jonathan as a "very straight dealer" but feared that he might have stumbled on a racket that involved stolen antiques being smuggled out of the country.

Jonathan had many friends in the antiques world. They spoke of him with great affection and saw him as "happy and honest". He was deeply in love with his wife and seemed to have everything to live for. Had he had an appointment with someone from the seedier side of the trade that night and come to some harm? A dozen antique dealers closed their shops for a day to help in the search for him.

Three agonizing days passed before any real news emerged. Jane gave what information she could to police at Littlehampton and details of the missing man

The sluice gates by the banks of the River Arun where Jonathan Lewis was dumped.

were published in local newspapers on the Thursday. Next morning the superintendent of Arundel swimming pool, Joe Pescott, read in the *West Sussex Gazette* that the police were looking for an orange Volvo. He had seen one such vehicle parked nearby for several days. The car that police had been scouring the county for was right there under their noses – in the pool car park directly opposite Arundel police station. Inside it, police found Jonathan's briefcase and an appointments book.

As soon as they heard about the discovery of the car, Colin and Jane decided to call at Arundel police station for a personal chat with the senior officer they knew, Superintendent Taylor. There they told him about their secret affair.

At about the same time two 16-year-old schoolboys enjoying a holiday trip in a speed boat were making their way up the Arun towards the Black Rabbit pub at Arundel when they spotted what looked like a head in the water. They summoned help from a fisherman who, armed with a gaff and some rope, managed with difficulty to tow the body about a mile and bring it inshore close to Ford Marina.

News of the find reached the police station while Colin and Jane were still there and it was Superintendent Taylor who had the unenviable task of taking Jane to one side and telling her that her husband's body had been found, in the river.

As Jonathan was known to have enjoyed walking his dog on the banks of the Arun, it was at first assumed that his death had been accidental. Initially the man in charge of the case, Detective Chief Inspector Gordon Harrison, Deputy Commander of west division CID based at Littlehampton, found no reason to disagree with that. A sum of £203 was found in a trouser pocket – so there had been no robbery – while the zip fly on his beige cord trousers was undone, as if to suggest that he had been spending a penny on the bank and had somehow slipped into the water.

Dr Iain West, the senior pathologist called in by police to examine the body, discovered that the victim had a fractured skull, though the only visible sign of injury was a gash to the forehead. He became sure that the injuries had been caused prior to death, and confirmed that death was almost certainly due to subsequent drowning.

Next day the newspapers published the official position: that the body of the missing antiques dealer had been found in the Arun, but that there were no suspicious circumstances.

During that same summer weekend, Harrison and some of his senior men were engaged in a search for a small child, Elizabeth Peck, who had vanished from her parents while picnicking at the Whiteways beauty spot to the north of Arundel.

A massive search of thick woodland and undergrowth involving 100 policemen was under way and the distraught parents and their two other children were being questioned at Arundel police station. The child was found alive and well after two days in the wild.

As a result of this other enquiry, it was not until Sunday morning that Harrison began looking more closely into the case of Jonathan Lewis. He met and talked to Jane and learned for the first time about the affair with Wallace. (Although Superintendent Taylor had been told on the Friday, there had been no discussion between the two men since then.) He thought it obvious that Jane had her suspicions of Colin.

He found, too, some unanswered questions. What had happened to the beige jacket Jonathan had been wearing that day? What had happened to his watch and a large bunch of keys? Was it possible that the cut on the head had been caused by an assailant?

Jonathan was no weakling. Weighing $13\frac{1}{2}$ stone, 5ft 11in tall, he was a very fit and agile 29-year-old who played squash three times a week and had been a very strong swimmer. Was he likely to have fallen into the river and drowned?

What intrigued Harrison more, however, was an entry in the dead man's appointments diary for August 5: it read simply "Colin 6.30 p.m." From new statements being gathered by his team of 20 detectives he knew that an Austin Princess car bearing distinctive "It's A Knockout" stickers and a Union Jack emblem had been seen in the vicinity of the pool car park at around that time on that day. Four of these vehicles had been supplied by car firm Wadham Stringer for use during the recording of the TV show, two being used by members of the BBC production team, one by tourism officer Ned Wayne and the other by Colin Wallace. The police now learned that one had already been returned, one had gone to Manchester and another had broken down, leaving only Wallace's still on the road in Arundel.

Inevitably suspicion fell on Colin Wallace. Two days after the body was found, early on Sunday evening, he went to Arundel police station to answer some questions. The questions centred upon that entry in Lewis's diary.

At the interview, Wallace made it clear that he and Jonathan were on good terms; they had played their regular game of squash on the Monday and had shared the secret of the surprise dinner party for Jane. He confirmed that Jonathan had called him at 4.20 p.m. on the Tuesday to say that he would probably be late for the dinner because of another appointment. The 6.30 entry in his diary? That was merely another squash game that they had decided to cancel.

Wallace signed a statement to this effect. Then Harrison told him that they had a witness who had seen one of the "It's a Knockout" cars near the pool car park at that time and also that a man answering Wallace's description had been seen to meet another man by the orange Volvo.

Suddenly the mood in the police station changed. Wallace bent his head forward, holding his face in his hand for a full two minutes, obviously deep in thought. When he looked up, he offered a completely different version of events.

His new story was that, yes, Jonathan had rung him on that Tuesday, but not in connection with the dinner; he had, in fact, asked to see Colin for a personal chat. They had met in the pool car park at 6.30 p.m. and driven in the Austin Princess to Wallace's home at Dalloway Road. On the way Jonathan said he had reason to believe that Colin and his wife were having an affair. Over a drink, Colin had told him that it was not an affair, but admitted that there was "a relationship" and that he was now seeking a job elsewhere as a result. It had been a dignified and amicable chat over gin and tonics and Jonathan had seemed to accept the situation. Afterwards he had simply taken him back into Arundel and dropped him in the town by the bridge at around 7.20, expecting to see him later at the dinner.

Wallace said that he had kept his meeting with Jonathan secret only because he desperately wanted to keep the affair with Jane private. The police, though, thought it odd that he had not told even Jane about the meeting with Jonathan, or revealed to anyone that he had seen the Volvo in the pool car park during the days that it was so urgently sought after.

Wallace's home at Dalloway Road was searched from top to bottom, forensic tests carried out and a bundle of his clothes taken away for inspection. The Austin Princess he had used was subjected to minute examination.

After two days with the police, Wallace was allowed to go home and returned to his work. The police investigation went on. A large photograph of Jonathan Lewis was displayed outside a mobile incident room in Arundel and any member of the public who had seen him on August 5, especially between 6.15 p.m. and 11.30, was asked to come forward. A white Austin Princess bearing "It's a Knockout" stickers and a Union Jack on the bonnet toured the streets in the hope that it might jog the memory of anyone who might have seen a similar car in the area of the pool and the banks of the Arun between Ford Marina and the Black Rabbit pub.

Detectives had discovered that the boot of Wallace's car had been thoroughly cleaned out and that its lining was missing. Now they were looking for a discarded boot lining.

Potential witnesses came forward in abundance, especially locals who had seen a car with the flag on the bonnet at various points around the town. A council cleaner, Maisie Blight, said she had seen a man cleaning out the boot of one such decorated vehicle behind the council offices in Littlehampton at around 6 a.m. on August 6 – the morning after Jonathan went missing. This was Colin Wallace – he did not deny it.

A woman taking her dog for a walk on the banks of the Arun, Phyllis Pointer, had found a damaged watch near the sluice gates at the end of a small track known as Gasworks Lane. It turned out to have belonged to Jonathan Lewis, a present to him from his mother on his 21st birthday, and it provided the clue to where he might have entered the fast-flowing water. A thorough search of this area, which is easily reached from the Arundel by-pass, revealed marks on the steep river bank that could have been made by a body sliding downwards. Just off the path, some distance from where the watch was found, a policeman recovered Jonathan's missing keys. The police became convinced that it was here that Jonathan went into the water, the movement of the tide taking his body back and fro some five times before it rose to the surface and was spotted near Ford Marina.

Meanwhile a second post-mortem on the body by Dr West had made significant discoveries. Dr West had concentrated on signs of injury around the nose and had found that, in addition to the forehead cut, Jonathan Lewis had suffered a rare type of facial injury that was extremely difficult to detect. He had received a fierce blow to the face which had rammed his nose backwards and upward, cracking the front of his skull. Dr West believed that this could have been caused with the heel of a hand and added that deep bruising across the nape of the neck and the back of the shoulders suggested that the attacker might well have pulled Lewis suddenly into the path of the blow. Or he might have been grabbed from behind and violently rammed forward into a solid object, perhaps a wall.

Although the injury was a vicious one by any standards, it would not have killed Lewis, though it would have left him severely concussed and probably unconscious for up to an hour. Had he recovered his senses before entering the river, he would have remained very groggy.

There was now no shred of doubt that Jonathan Lewis's death had not been accidental. On Friday, August 15, a week after Lewis's body had been recovered from the Arun, the head of Sussex CID, Chief Superintendent Charles Johnstone, made a dramatic new public announcement. For the first time he stated officially that he was leading a full-scale murder enquiry. He told a press conference: "We are not looking for a murder weapon but I am not able to tell you the reason why. I am now quite satisfied that Mr Lewis was murdered."

Wallace had already spent 48 uncomfortable hours at the police station. His apprehension must have been even more acute still when, on August 23, Detective Chief Inspector Harrison called him in for another chat about his movements on August 5, revealing to him that police forensic tests had now discovered considerable evidence of blood staining in the boot of the Austin Princess that he had been using. Three weeks later, on the evening of September 18, Harrison appeared again at Wallace's door to take him once more to Littlehampton police station.

The next day, Friday, September 19, was to have been a special one in Wallace's calendar. He was taking his wife out for dinner to celebrate her birthday while the edited film of the Arundel "It's a Knockout" show was going out on BBC TV at 7.00 p.m. He missed both occasions. Instead, he was brought before Arundel Magistrates Court charged with the killing of his friend Jonathan Lewis.

The considerable respect that Wallace had won in his Arun post was evident during the court hearing, which was attended by the Duke of Norfolk, then Earl Marshal of England, the Mayor of Littlehampton, and the Arun Council's solicitor and secretary, Philip Owens – all prepared to stand bail for Wallace. The magistrates, however, remanded him in custody to Lewes Gaol, where he remained for two months.

When the case was committed for trial on December 1 another request to have Wallace released on bail was refused by the same magistrates, but his solicitor James Morgan-Harris successfully applied to a judge in chambers for his client to be freed from custody on bail of £4,000, which was speedily supplied by his friends in high places.

Suspended on full pay from his job, Wallace spent that Christmas at home with his wife Eileen. Hardly celebrating, but preparing a Not Guilty plea for Lewes Crown Court.

The allegation against him was spelled out by prosecuting counsel Dan Hollis Q.C. when the trial opened on Tuesday, March 3, 1981. "You could say this was the case of the man who never came to dinner," he began grimly.

Hollis alleged that Wallace had planned the killing because of his love for Jonathan's wife. He had arranged for his wife to play squash with Jane early on the evening of August 5 and for the two women to go straight to the Avisford Park Hotel. In the meantime he had set up the secret meeting with Jonathan.

While they were talking over drinks at Dalloway Road between 6.30 and 7.15 p.m. Wallace had chosen his moment to lash out a fierce blow, rendering him unconscious. The actual location was not certain, but this might have happened when Jonathan had visited the downstairs toilet or the upstairs bathroom.

He had dragged the body through the house into the rear of the garage then crammed it into the boot of the Austin Princess, which he had reversed into the drive to be ready. With the unconscious man in the car, he had, at some stage during that evening, driven the Princess to Gasworks Lane just off the Arundel by-pass and reversed the vehicle down to the banks of the Arun. There he had hauled Jonathan out and pushed him down a steep concrete-lined bank into the fast-flowing river, close to the old sluice gates. As he had dragged him across the rough ground, the victim's watch had been ripped off and his keys had fallen out of a pocket.

One of the other courtesy cars used by the police in their appeal for further information and witnesses.

This may have happened between 7.00 p.m. and 8.00 p.m. as Wallace was on his way to join guests at the hotel dinner, or it might have taken place later in the evening, under the cover of darkness, when he had made an excuse to leave the table at about 10.30 p.m.

When Wallace had returned to the hotel, he had feigned sympathy over the missing man, pretended to assist in the search and early next morning had given the boot a thorough clean out, dumping the boot lining and possibly the jacket too.

It all fitted neatly into place. Or did it?

The trial became something of an Agatha Christie whodunit. At times the central theme of the prosecution shone through powerfully, especially during the police evidence and to some extent with the appearance of Jane Lewis, whose affection for her boss had turned to suspicion of him. There were other times of great doubt as new trails suddenly opened up, then closed again. There were red herrings galore.

Wallace strongly denied the allegations throughout, while his counsel, Michael Kennedy Q.C. knocked more than just a few holes in the prosecution case. He contended that the two men had always been on good terms, that the accused was not a man capable of serious violence and had not been involved in the death in any way. "We suggest that the evidence as a whole in fact shows that he is innocent of this charge and that if you cut your way through suspicious speculation and sheer fantasy you will see this is the truth," he told the jury. "The true position as to these injuries is that anybody could have caused them."

There was an alternative scenario that would equally fit the facts, Kennedy pointed out: Lewis could have been attacked some time after 7.20 p.m. while walking by the Arun, left unconscious and later staggered down to the river, maybe to urinate, fallen in and drowned.

More than fifty prosecution witnesses were paraded before the court during the thirteen-day hearing. Some did comfortably fit the prosecution story, however others clearly did not. The average observer might have been excused for wondering why they had been called.

There were numerous car spotters who had seen a "Knockout" Princess on August 5 – so many in fact that not all of them could have been correct. There was Mrs Ryder, the lady from the squash club, who had telephoned the Wallace house on the fateful evening of August 5. She put the call at just before 8.00 p.m. Wallace had timed it at 7.15 p.m. One of them was wrong.

Then there was the mysterious Mr Y, the shady figure from the world of antiques whom Jane Lewis had been warned to watch out for by her dead husband. His name was written down on a slip of paper for the jury, but nothing more learned of him.

There was the bass fisherman Douglas Hart, who had seen a mysterious light near the sluice gates just after midnight and veteran boatman Andre Buller who doubted that a body dumped there could have reached the Ford area in three days.

One of the most puzzling and disturbing of these witnesses was Amanda Metcalfe whose parents ran the Golden Goose public house near Arundel railway station. Following the police appeal, she had come forward to declare that she had seen Jonathan Lewis drinking at the bar with another man after 7.00 p.m. on August 5.

She gave an uncannily accurate description of the clothes that Lewis was wearing on that day, right down to his "chocolate-coloured" socks. And she was convinced that she had the time and date right because she had stayed on to assist a new barman named Vince. She did not recognize the other man, and did not think it was Wallace.

If this was true then Lewis could not have been attacked at Dalloway Road between 6.30 p.m. and 7.15 p.m. It was a vital testimony, yet didn't fit the rest of the jigsaw. The police view was that Miss Metcalfe was an honest witness, but mistaken.

With all of the evidence against Wallace circumstantial, the forensic information became critical. The court learned that the detailed search of the house at Dalloway Road had produced nothing apart from a minute spot of what might have been blood in the upstairs toilet. It was therefore the presence of blood in the boot of the car that occupied a vital part of the court's attention, prompting a long and complex clash between defence and prosecution.

This evidence was highly technical and extremely difficult for the layman to follow. However one thing stood out vividly. Metropolitan Police expert Leslie Silverman revealed that Lewis's blood group was very rare, occurring in only 1.6 per cent of the population, and that among the 20 spots of blood found in the car boot some were from that exceptional group.

But forensic analysis is rarely cut and dried. Silverman also made it apparent that some of the blood stains could not be typed and this raised the disconcerting likelihood that more than one person had bled into this brand-new car. The police had done their best to track down everyone who had travelled in the vehicle, including Eddie Waring from the BBC, but not even a nose bleed had been traced.

As the prosecution case concluded, Wallace's counsel made a bid to persuade the judge, Mr Justice Kilner Brown, that there was no case to answer and that the hearing should be terminated there and then. For several hours the jury were excluded from the courtroom as the judge discussed the legal position with Kennedy and Hollis.

The ploy failed to win favour, the judge preferring that the jury should decide on the quality of evidence and not he. However what came next caused ripples of astonishment throughout the court and a major sensation for the gathered journalists. Judge Brown declared that there was insufficient evidence to continue on the murder charge; instead, he instructed the jury to try the defendant on a charge of manslaughter. His decision rested on a legal distinction. To put an unconscious man into water, so that he drowns, is murder; to put a man whom you think to be already dead, but isn't, into water is manslaughter. The scientific evidence was that Lewis was still alive when he went into the Arun, but the judge

Colin Wallace

had concluded from the prosecution presentation that the assailant could have believed Lewis to be dead when he dumped him in the river. Therefore it could not be murder.

Wallace himself was on the stand for more than four hours, during which the attention of the press bench was drawn to his past links with the SAS. The headlines next day were predictably lurid and many of them were linked to a rare photograph of Wallace wearing full parachute rig plus cap complete with a New Zealand SAS insignia.

This image of a tough soldier could hardly have been to Wallace's advantage while allegations were being bandied about in court of a rare "pile-driver" punch being inflicted on the victim. Kennedy did his utmost to dispel any doubts in the minds of the jury by asking Wallace: "Have you ever received any form of close combat or similar training, or any sort of karate training?" To which the reply was "No, I have not."

Jane Lewis

Wallace produced an explanation for everything. He said that he had suffered stomach trouble for years and that his absence from the dinner to take tablets was quite genuine. After leaving Dalloway Road he had been concerned that Jonathan had not turned up for the meal and returned to the pool car park to see if the Volvo was still there. It was.

This might have explained his 40 minutes absence from the table, but of course this was vital information that he had withheld from his friends and the police all through the days of searching for a missing man. That cannot have gone down at all well with the jury, and must have helped seal his fate.

Wallace then had to parry some tough cross-examination from Hollis, which he did solidly.

"You have no idea how he got his nose pushed up to his skull so his skull fractured?" asked the prosecutor. Answer: "No".

"Are you familiar with a blow with the heel of the palm of the hand as demonstrated by Dr West?" Answer: "No, I am not".

Hollis suggested to him that he did not tell the dinner party that he had seen Jonathan Lewis earlier that evening "because you knew that he never would turn up for dinner. That is the truth of the matter isn't it?" Wallace: "No, that is not true".

Three car assembly workers from the British Leyland factory at Cowley, Brian Weaver, Robin Shrewsbury and Mabu Allam, gave evidence for the defence. With stories backed up by medical records, they told the court how they had sustained cuts while assembling the Austin Princess on June 6, 1979. Blood from at least one of them might have found its way into the critical boot area.

This was an ingenious piece of detective work by Wallace's lawyers. It explained the variety of blood groups in the car. Could anyone now rely on the blood-in-the-boot theory as a serious part of the Crown case?

The jury spent 4 hours and 26 minutes deliberating that and the many other conundrums hurled at them during a remarkable 13-day trial. They dismissed the evidence of Miss Metcalfe's sighting at the Golden Goose and they chose not to believe Wallace's denials. The unanimous verdict: guilty of manslaughter.

The Judge jailed Colin Wallace for ten years and took the opportunity to deliver a stern homily:

This was a dreadful case, a horrifying case. There was a perfectly innocent man, a man on the verge of being cuckolded by you and that man received these savage blows. It may well be that you believed he was dead. It may well be that you could not care one way or the other. In my judgement one has got to recognise that there had never been an attempt to explain what happened. The very notion of driving that body and tipping it into the river revolts the human consciousness. As manslaughter goes, in my experience, it is one of the worst cases I have come across.

After his appeal failed, Wallace settled down to serve five years of the term behind bars. He was said to be a model prisoner. He was released in 1986. The campaign to clear his name began well before then, led by his own driving determination but also steadfastly supported by his wife Eileen, who has stoutly declared his innocence ever since.

"My husband is no killer", she told a journalist, "and one day we shall prove it. He was framed to gag him".

The Wallace case has become one of the most sensational in Sussex history, and if Mrs Wallace is right then there are more remarkable chapters yet unwritten.

However, the defiant wife was wrong on one account. Even when they put

Jonathan Lewis

him behind bars, her husband was never effectively gagged.

Colin Wallace has gone on talking, researching and compiling reports which have continued to arouse the attention of journalists and politicians in a quite extraordinary fashion until the January of 1990 when his case was once more blazoned across the front pages of national newspapers and occupied prime TV news time.

Armed with a massive dossier, prepared while in jail, he had stalked the corridors of power at Westminster, lobbied Ministers and cajoled MPs with a series of startling and sensational allegations which, for some, had seemed too outrageous to be true.

His two declared ambitions were to establish that he was unfairly dismissed by the Army in June 1975 and that he was not involved in the manslaughter of Jonathan Lewis in the August of 1980.

Both of these calamities in his life were inflicted on him, he claimed, in order to discredit him, and prevent the spreading of his vital knowledge of the notorious Clockwork Orange campaign whose secret activities are said to have included the under-mining of not only the forces of terrorism but numerous leading British politicians of the 70s.

At first, people listened, but few believed. Denials that the clandestine Clockwork Orange operation ever existed flowed from Whitehall.

Apparently not in the least bit daunted by rejection, Wallace turned to various MPs who were prepared to bombard the Commons with questions and to the Daily Mirror journalist Paul Foot who in 1989 published a highly provocative book on the subject.

Eventually – and miraculously – someone inside the Ministry of Defence unearthed documents, hitherto thought not to exist, which convinced certain members of the civil service that, certainly in the case of his departure from the Army, Wallace might just have a point.

Early in 1990 Prime Minister Mrs Thatcher was forced to make a statement in which she has said that previous denials were incorrect while armed forces minister Archie Hamilton confirmed that "inaccurate statements" had been made in the Commons.

Physchological warfare against terrorism had existed in Northern Ireland, although 'not against politicians', it was conceded. The circumstances of Mr Wallace's dismissal became the subject of an official inquiry by a leading lawyer, Thomas Calcutt QC, while a Commons Select Committee on Defence was ordered to inquire into the wider allegations of smears against politicians.

After an extensive investigation into Wallace's employment with the Army, Calcutt concluded in September 1990 that his 1975 appeal against dismissal had been "unsatisfactory" and he was awarded £30,000 by way of compensation.

This remarkable turn of events helped to paint a wholly new picture of the Wallace who had been regularly dismissed in some quarters as a "Walter Mitty" character. If what he was saying about his startling army career was turning out to be correct, then could not his other claims be true as well?

The new developments established that Wallace was part of a cloak and dagger under-cover operation, a member of a unit which apparently specialised in the spreading of black propaganda.

His second 'goal' – to clear his name of manslaughter – remained unresolved in 1990 because The Home Office did not consider that there were any new grounds to re-investigate.

But one thing is certain: Mr Wallace is not a man content to give up at that.

8
THE BODY IN THE BOOT
The Murder of James Sergeant, 1984

James Sergeant was a handsome and always well-dressed young man. Tall, with the athletic physique of the regular squash player, he patronized fashionable hairdressers and wore smart, casual clothes – usually with an expensive watch at his wrist and a prominent gold chain around his neck. He liked fast cars – within five years he owned in succession a Triumph TR6, a Jaguar, a Pontiac Firebird and a Chevrolet Blazer. He liked women, and seemed to have no difficulty attracting them.

He came from a close knit Surrey family, and, at 28, still lived at home with his father and a brother in a large country house, the Knoll, at Lower Kingswood, near Reigate – though he was often absent for long periods.

He never seemed to be short of money, although he had no regular job. Sometimes he worked as a night club bouncer, but he was really a wheeler-dealer – an Arthur Daley of the Surrey-Sussex borders. He traded in second-hand cars and in electrical goods, clothes and jewellery – the sort of things that may fall off the back of a lorry. Some people suggested that he also dealt in drugs, but Sussex police never found any evidence of this.

Why he was murdered in the summer of 1984 is still not known. And who killed him remains one of the most baffling mysteries currently left open on the files of the Sussex Constabulary.

It began with the discovery of his body – in a way that might have come straight out of fiction.

A friend of his, a pretty 22 year-old sales executive named Lisa Mansfield, had lent him her metallic maroon Volkswagen Derby while his own car was off the road. Sergeant had stayed at Lisa's home in Sutton, Surrey, on Thursday, August 23, 1984. On the following morning he had dropped her at work and driven off in the Derby.

Lisa looked forward to seeing him again and to getting her car back – apart from anything else he had promised to fix its faulty boot lock. But the days passed and he did not return. At first she was not worried – Jimmy was always a man with a full diary. But when two weeks passed with no news, even her patience was stretched and on September 5 she rang the Knoll. She spoke to Jimmy's father, who said that he had not seen his son for nearly a fortnight. He thought Jimmy must be in Spain – he had been talking about visiting a friend who was staying there. Perhaps if Lisa wanted her car back, she should try looking at Gatwick Airport.

Miraculously, among the thousands of cars at this busy international airport, Lisa spotted her own, standing in row 2 of level 3 of short-stay car park number 2. But she could not drive it away because she had no spare ignition key. She went to the Knoll and talked to Jimmy's brother, Andrew.

Then someone noticed an obnoxious odour coming from the car and, at just past midnight on Thursday, September 6, officers wearing protective clothing and face masks forced opened its boot. Inside, wrapped in a blanket, they found the body of a young man, the torso riddled by shotgun pellets. The fingerprints, sent to police headquarters in Lewes in the early hours of the morning, established that it was that of James Rufus Sergeant, a man already known to the police for minor offences. He had been reported missing two days before.

The manner of Sergeant's death was revealed by the post-mortem.

A blast of shot from a 12-gauge shotgun had torn a hole 2½" in diameter in his stomach and left 346 pellets of various sizes embedded in the wound. The shot had been fired from between six and ten feet away. Sergeant went down on one knee, clutching at his stomach. His attacker closed in and fired a second shot from only two feet away, this time – judging from the angle at which the pellets entered his right upper arm – standing over him. A third shot, fired into Sergeant's back, blasted pellets right through his chest into his right forearm. The attacker must have stopped to reload between the shots.

Experts concluded that the first wound had been "extremely painful and instantly disabling" but that, although it had caused "severe damage", it had not been immediately fatal. Neither had the second and third wounds. Sergeant could have been saved, given medical treatment. But he had been allowed to die in agony.

A team of 40 Sussex detectives led by Detective Superintendent Douglas Cheal set out to find the killer, operating from a murder room in the Gatwick Airport police station.

They were the first major enquiry team to use the Sussex police's sophisticated new mini-computer, the Triton Four. Police in Yorkshire had been severely criticized for allowing themselves to become submerged by mountains of paper and lost leads during the Yorkshire Ripper enquiry. Triton Four was one of the two computer systems that the Home Office had, after that debacle, approved to replace the old, cumbersome card-index system. It had already helped detectives working in Bedfordshire to track down the notorious rapist known as "the Fox".

Without the new technology, the big Sussex murder team would have been swamped by the volume of information that came in. Soon hundreds of statements, addresses, telephone numbers and descriptions were being entered into the computer, so that any required information could be retrieved at the touch of a button.

From interviews with Sergeant's friends and relatives the police were able to build up a picture of his last-known movements. No-one could recall having seen him since Friday, August 24. But on that day he had been very active indeed. He had been seen by several people at three different locations – Purley Squash Club, the East Surrey Hospital in Redhill and the Plough Inn at Rusper.

He had gone to the squash club near the A23 Brighton road between 6.00 p.m. and 6.30 p.m. He had then been wearing grey track-suit trousers, a white T-shirt and training shoes. Between 8.00 p.m. and 8.30 p.m. he had been in the out-patient suite on the first floor of the Redhill hospital, receiving treatment for an abscess on his left thigh. Later in the evening, wearing different casual clothes, he had been drinking – and in high spirits – at the Plough. His friends were fairly sure that he had been driving the Volkswagen Derby all evening.

Many people remembered Sergeant in the Plough, a popular 300-year-old village pub, because he had been flaunting a wad of notes. He had on him between £1,500 and £2,000 in £50 notes, the proceeds from the sale of a jeep to a dealer in Brighton.

Landlord Tony Cripps remembered the evening well. He and his wife, Denise, were celebrating their wedding anniversary, and for the first time in weeks he decided not to serve behind the bar but to join his customers on the other side. He found himself sitting opposite Sergeant, who stood out because he was wearing denim Levi shorts, something Cripps and his wife did not normally approve of on their premises. He watched as Sergeant splashed out on drinks for himself and two other young men and saw the wad of notes. A former London publican with more than 30 years in the trade, he said he had never seen a wad as large in a pub. He took Sergeant to one side to warn him of the risk he was taking in letting it be known that he had a lot of money on him. Sergeant had simply stuffed the money into the back pocket of his shorts.

Sergeant's drinking companions were two of his friends, Simon Rundle and Robert Lloyd.

Lloyd, from Redhill, was an intelligent young man who had some interests in common with Sergeant – he shared, for example, his companion's enthusiasm for high-performance cars. His other hobbies included fishing and shooting – he owned a set of rods and two shotguns. Unlike Sergeant, he had a regular, well-paid job – as a casino croupier – and, again unlike Sergeant, he was a family man. His wife, Michelle, was an attractive ex-model and they had two young children.

Rundle, a welder and car mechanic from Tadworth, was another old mate. He joined with the other two in the evening's ribaldry and horseplay. He remembered that when he had offered to stand his round, Sergeant had ribbed him about the small amount of money had had in his wallet and flashed his own roll of notes, boasting that he had "double the amount".

When the little drinking party broke up soon after 10.00 p.m., the men were all in a lively mood. According to Rundle, Sergeant was "staggering drunk" and Lloyd "fairly sober" when they left the pub. The landlord, though, thought that Lloyd "had far more under his belt than he could possibly hold." A woman in the bar who had been bought a drink by Sergeant said that he was "jovial and high spirited".

What happened to Sergeant after he left the Plough that evening remains a mystery.

He was to have picked up another acquaintance, radio engineer Bruce Huddlestone, in Epsom at 10.15 p.m. and to have gone with him to Scarletts night club in Purley. Afterwards Sergeant intended to go on to Stringfellows in London to spend more of his big windfall.

Huddlestone waited, but Sergeant never turned up. He must have been gunned down sometime later that night.

MURDER

THE **BODY** OF JAMES RUFUS SARGEANT AGE 28 YEARS
WAS **FOUND IN** THE ABOVE **CAR** AT
GATWICK AIRPORT ON WEDNESDAY 5th SEPTEMBER

HE WAS **LAST SEEN**
ON THE EVENING OF FRIDAY **24**th **AUGUST**
IN THE **THE PLOUGH** PUBLIC HOUSE AT **RUSPER**

DID YOU SEE HIM OR **THE CAR**
BETWEEN THOSE TIMES

IF YOU DID PLEASE CONTACT THE INCIDENT ROOM
AT GATWICK POLICE STATION TEL: CRAWLEY 36602
OR CRAWLEY 31122

The police poster issued by Sussex C.I.D.

E

Mobile incident room set up by police at Rusper.

The little community of Rusper, with just 1,220 people on the electoral roll, became the focal point of the police investigation. Working from a mobile incident room set up in the quaint High Street, officers pinned up posters seeking help and began extensive house-to-house enquiries.

One resident recalled hearing two shots, about three seconds apart, at about 1.00 a.m. However, that lead was one of several that went nowhere and police had to reconcile themselves to the fact that quite a number of folk in the countryside shoot game during the night.

If the police could recover the murder weapon, it could tell them much about the killer. Another report of gunshots heard that night sent a team of police frogmen to search the River Mole at Three Bridges, but they did not find the gun.

On the evening of Friday, September 7, two days after the discovery of Sergeant's body, detectives joined regular drinkers at the Plough, hoping to learn more about his final movements. They traced 35 people who had been in the pub on the fatal night. The mountain of computerized data began to grow, but progress was admittedly slow.

Appeals to the public for fresh information continued for two months. The

Sergeant family was becoming concerned about the lack of results and another brother, John, put up a £10,000 reward for information that might lead to an arrest and conviction.

As more weeks slipped by with no significant progress being made, the family staged a press conference at Gatwick on October 22 and announced that the reward would be increased to £50,000. The offer was said at the time to be the highest ever made by private individuals for the conviction of a criminal. The dead man's father, 77-year-old Arthur Sergeant, told journalists: "We are not looking for revenge, how can we have revenge for someone's life? All we want is justice".

Detective Superintendent Cheal, who by then had his own ideas about who the killer was, said he hoped the new reward would encourage people with "vital information" to come forward.

The police especially wanted to talk to more people who knew the dead man or who had seen him on August 24. They issued a distinctive snapshot of him and described the clothing he was last seen wearing – denim shorts, white socks, a grey sleeveless T-shirt and a copper bracelet. They were also anxious to learn of any sightings of the car, registration number GGC 646T, either between Rusper and Gatwick or, better still, being parked at Gatwick.

Detectives were also looking for the ticket that the car's driver must have drawn to obtain access to the car park and for the car keys, which were believed to be on a ring with six others, belonging to the dead man. And they hoped to find someone who would recognize the old beige wool blanket in which the body had been wrapped; it was 6ft 2in square, with yellow, silk-like edging on two sides.

After completing their house-to-house enquiries, the detectives tried to trace everyone who had been in the busy Gatwick car park between 10.30 p.m. and 3.00 a.m. on the night of August 24/25. They felt sure that someone must have seen the Volkswagen entering and the driver leaving.

But they drew a series of blanks. No-one had seen the driver of the Volkswagen Derby arrive or depart from the airport. The keys were never found. The gun never recovered. The blanket never identified.

Of major significance, of course, was the absence of money on the victim. Some of the money from the jeep deal he had spent in the Plough, but most must have been still in his pocket when left. Now it was missing. So robbery emerged as a prime motive.

But there were other possibilities that could not be ignored. Sergeant's wheeling and dealing might well have brought him into contact with organized criminals. It was possible that he had fallen foul of the rackets, some of which thrive in Brighton. Might it be a gangland killing?

Or was Sergeant involved in the Brighton drugs traffic? His drinking companion Simon Rundle, when he later appeared in court as a witness, accused Sergeant of being mixed up in a drugs business, claiming that he supplied "speed" to users in Sussex through regular meetings at the Plough. Rundle said that he himself had bought from Sergeant drugs worth £60 or £70, at meetings at the Plough. Another of the dead man's acquaintances, tractor driver Reginald Brooks, claimed that Sergeant took the amphetamine pills known as "blues". These allegations did not escape the attention of the Sussex drugs squad, but they never became important to the murder team and no evidence emerged to suggest that Sergeant was either a drug dealer or a user.

So did the key to the mystery lie in Sergeant's love affairs? As police pieced together a picture of his colourful life, they learned that he had enjoyed a large number of affairs with single and married women. Officers spoke to six different women, two of whom were married, who claimed to have had relationships with him during the previous twelve months. Two former girl-friends, one of them living north of London, had responded to the appeals for help by providing "useful information" to the Gatwick incident room.

"We are working on a jigsaw", Detective Inspector Sparks said at one stage. "One tiny piece of information which appears insignificant on its own can help us complete the picture of what happened". But that piece was still missing. Detective Superintendent Cheal admitted that "for various reasons a number of witnesses have been reluctant to come forward and give information. People do not want to get involved, possibly they have got previous convictions or maybe they are too embarrassed." Or, he added, some people might be too scared – after all, a vicious killer was still at large.

The police enquiry continued into November and continued to make no headway, but all the time, from a very early stage, there had been one prime suspect and now the police involvement with him, which had counterpointed the investigation, came to a head. The suspect was Sergeant's old friend, and drinking companion on the fatal night, Robert Lloyd.

He had been among the last to see James Sergeant alive. He was familiar with shotguns. And detectives discovered that his attractive wife Michelle was among the women who had had a relationship with Sergeant.

As soon as this became known to the police, they wanted to interview Robert

Lloyd, but, to their acute embarrassment, they learned that Michelle, Robert and their two children had gone on holiday to Spain. The Gatwick-based team simply had to wait patiently for their return.

Meanwhile they made what investigations they could. They received total co-operation from other members of the Lloyd family. Those close to the heart of the matter could detect at that time the intensity of feeling that was running through the two families chiefly concerned – the Sergeants, determined to obtain justice for their dead son and the Lloyds, equally anxious to ensure that their son obtained fair treatment from the law.

Lloyd's parents agreed to attend as observers when detectives gained a search warrant to go through the empty Lloyd home at Greenwood Drive in Redhill. They watched as men scoured the house, finally taking away for forensic testing a variety of items, including some unused French-made shotgun cartridges of a rare type. They interested the police because two types of lead shot had been found in Sergeant's body – number 6 and, in his chest, number 3. The number-3 shot was according to the forensic experts, similar in weight to the French number-4 shot in the cartridges in Lloyd's house.

Another member of the family, Robert's brother Thomas, offered his assistance following the public appeal for information, inviting members of the enquiry team on to his land at Woodland Farm in the tiny Surrey village of Newdigate, where on a lonely track, the Lloyds often practised shooting using a variety of shotguns. Indeed, the brothers had been doing just that only a matter of days before August 24. Also on the land was a large caravan in which the family kept various items of equipment, including fishing tackle and shotguns.

Woodland Farm was only a matter of a mile or two to the north of Rusper, via the back lanes, and police interest in the farm became intense. At one stage they brought in a leading forensic scientist.

On Sunday, September 23, detectives waited for the arrival of a charter flight from Spain at Gatwick Airport. Robert and Michelle Lloyd were approached just after clearing customs and invited to "assist with inquiries", while their surprised children were escorted elsewhere.

Michelle was allowed to go after a few hours, but her husband remained at Horsham police station for the next three days – arrested on suspicion of murder.

During questioning by Detective Inspector David Wood, Lloyd was shown what were called "distressing" photographs of Sergeant's body and it was suggested to him that he was the man the police sought. But he repeatedly denied any involvement in the killing and steadfastly stuck to this position.

Lloyd was given police bail and released on September 26. As far as the public and press were concerned, they knew nothing of this arrest and merely understood that a man had been assisting with enquiries, but was no longer detained.

A week later, on Friday, November 2, Lloyd returned voluntarily to the police station to face another three days of "exhaustive" questioning. Once more he strenuously denied any knowledge of the killing. During the Saturday, Athony Blok, a lawyer called in to advise Lloyd, warned the police that if his client was kept in custody any longer he would be entitled to claim unlawful imprisonment – there is a strict limit to the time any person can be held inside a police station for questioning.

Lloyd made one more brief statement to Detective Inspector Wood: "I feel I have been asked enough questions and given enough answers to help you in your investigations. If you feel it is right to charge me with an offence, you charge me. I would like you to either charge me or release me."

When Wood replied that enquiries were continuing and that he could not say when Lloyd would be released, Mr Blok moved to the High Court in London when he lodged a writ of habeas corpus. On the Monday morning, November 5, a judge ordered the police to release Lloyd by 6.00 p.m. that day.

The Sussex police were forced now either to free Lloyd or charge him. They decided that they had gone too far to turn back and Robert Lloyd was formally charged with the murder of his friend James Sergeant.

The wheels of justice, as always, took an exceedingly long time to turn. Robert Lloyd was held in custody at Lewes Prison over Christmas 1984 and the first months of 1985. In March of that year, Crawley magistrates, after listening to five days of evidence, committed Lloyd for trial. He went back to prison and finally appeared before Lewes Crown Court in the November of 1985, twelve months after the charge and a full fifteen months after the killing.

With the stage finally set, the prosecutor, David Cocks, Q.C., and defending counsel Robin Simpson found themselves agreeing on only one matter – both described the events leading up to the killing as "a weird story."

Mr Cocks spelled out the Crown case: "The motive for this killing was the classical one of revenge stirred up by jealousy that the dead man had had an affair with the defendant's wife". He alleged that Lloyd had lured Sergeant to Woodlands Farm after they had left the Plough by dangling before him the prospect of a deal over the sale of some stereo equipment and fishing tackle stored in the caravan on the farm. Once in the caravan Lloyd had produced a gun, shot

Robert Lloyd is led away after being charged with the murder by senior investigating officers. *(West Sussex County Times)*

The police incident room at Gatwick. The newly installed Home Office computer system is visible in the background.

Sergeant at close range, wrapped the body in a blanket and then dumped it a short car journey away at Gatwick Airport.

Among the few things found on the body, the court was told, had been a slip of paper on which were written details of a motorcycle, of some Pioneer stereo equipment and of some fishing tackle – presumably notes for some sort of deal.

Lloyd agreed that he had met Sergeant at Redhill hospital on August 24 and gone on with him to the Plough. He also agreed that he had given Sergeant some details of a motorcycle but said that he had had no intention of selling it to Sergeant – in fact, one of his reasons for going to the pub that evening had been to try and sell it to Rundle. Certainly, he had bought some stereo equipment from Sergeant at one time. And he had some fishing tackle at his home in Redhill, and his father kept some in the caravan at Newdigate, but neither was up for sale, and he had no idea why fishing tackle should appear on Sergeant's note.

He and Sergeant had left the pub together, in jovial mood, and Sergeant had driven him, in the Volkswagen Derby, home to Redhill. He had dropped him off sometime between 10.15 p.m. and 10.30 p.m., saying he was going on to Brighton. He had not seen Sergeant since, and he flatly denied any knowledge of, or involvement in, the killing.

The hearing lasted for three weeks. Eighty witnesses were called. The prosecution case – it had been obvious from the beginning – hinged on circumstantial evidence, a possible motive and little else. There were no witnesses to the shooting and the gun could not be produced. Most of the essential facts were clouded in disagreement.

The single issue that was not in dispute was the affair between James Sergeant and Michelle Lloyd. After the two men had first become friendly, through their interest in fast cars and a mutual contact at a Merstham garage to the north of Redhill, Sergeant was quickly attracted to Michelle, and his feelings were reciprocated for a period of several months. At Christmas 1983 Michelle left a present for Sergeant at the Merstham garage. They met at nightclubs, and when Michelle and her next-door neighbour, Barbara Lennox, spent a winter holiday together in Scotland, Sergeant went along too.

Sergeant's sister, off-licence manageress Sonya Gaynor-Whitmore, told the court that her brother felt "very deeply" for Michelle and that when their affair eventually ended in the summer of 1984 he was very depressed about it.

It was not long before Robert Lloyd got a hint of what was going on. Michelle's aunt Sheila Connolly was at the Lloyd's house in Redhill in May 1984 when a bunch of flowers from Sergeant arrived for Michelle's birthday. In a fit of jealous anger, Lloyd threw them outside.

It was also suggested in court that Lloyd had bugged the telephone to find out what was going on. Sheila Connolly told of conversations she had with Lloyd: "He said he knew what was going on between Michelle and Jimmy Sergeant and I think he was upset about it. He said he would like to give Jimmy a hiding." But she also said that Lloyd was "always very cool" and "not in a temper in any way whatsoever".

It was Michelle who ended the affair. On the evening of July 27, she, Barbara Lennox and another friend, Donna Green, were at Scarletts night club together. Sergeant was working on the door. Michelle ignored him and spent a good deal of time chatting at the bar to a disc jockey named Steve Foweraker, who told the court that he had a month-long association with her during that July. He understood that her affair with Sergeant was over and that she and her husband were contemplating divorce. The three women left the club at about 3.00 a.m., passing Sergeant at the door.

Next morning Sergeant dumped a collection of bouquets, underwear and private love letters from Michelle on the roof of the Lloyds' car, which was standing outside their Redhill Home. Later in the morning he rang Lloyd to tell him to go out and look at the car. Later still the two men met and Sergeant showed Lloyd a diary recording every time he and Michelle had been together.

During his interviews with police, Lloyd admitted that the incident had upset him. "It was a natural reaction", he told Inspector Wood, who asked "Surely when you found your wife was having an affair you were jealous?" "No", Lloyd replied, "that is not so because from the day I found out the three of us spoke about it together and from that day I know she has not seen the chap."

He said that, although he had been suspicious before this incident, he had not been certain until then that Michelle was having an affair. He thought that Sergeant threw the items over the car to hurt Michelle, who had cold-shouldered him at the club the previous evening. He went on:

Afterwards I arranged to meet him at Earlswood Common. He tried to explain to me what had happened. He said he was sorry. He had had time to think about the damage he had done and he hoped it had not affected my children. He said he had lost my friendship. He was genuinely sorry and asked if there was anything he could do to help. He said it was all over as from now.

Inspector Wood then asked: "Are you really trying to say you took it that calmly, that you were not incensed by what had happened?" Lloyd replied: "I was annoyed. I spoke to Michelle and after finding it was finished we decided to try to put our marriage back on the right tracks." Sergeant and he "remained friendly", but he agreed "we were not as close as we had been."

The prosecution relied heavily on this question of motive and they were also pinning much on two "confessions" that Lloyd was alleged to have made, one during his long meetings with Wood at the police station and another with a cellmate at Lewes Prison.

The police inspector told the court that he had a conversation with Lloyd in a cell at Horsham in which Lloyd told him: "It was me or him, you know. You don't know what kind of a bastard he was." Lloyd denied that anything of the sort had ever happened. His counsel, Mr Simpson, suggested that Wood, under "enormous pressure", had invented the conversation. "When human beings are under pressure, the capacity of the human mind to convince itself something was said which they desperately want to believe was said is infinite," he declared.

Lloyd's cellmate in Lewes prison had been Gary Scott. The prosecution thought his evidence so important that he was flown in from Lisbon, where he was now living. He told the court: "I believe I said something like 'Did you really kill the man?' and he said 'yes'. It was something to do with drugs to start with, some money involved – he said he had been ripped off so much money by the bloke he killed. He said a few thousand pounds." Scott said he had asked Lloyd what it had felt like to kill Sergeant and he had replied there was "no feeling at all".

But under Simpson's cross-examination, Scott admitted that he had lived "a life of crime" and since 1974 had been found guilty of a number of offences of burglary, theft, dishonest handling and obtaining by deception, receiving sentences that ranged from a supervision order to Borstal training and finally prison. "You have a total and utter contempt for the law," declared the defence counsel. Simpson suggested that when Scott spoke to a police officer about Lloyd's alleged confession he had in mind an appeal that he was planning to lodge against his own sentence for burglary. However, Scott denied that. Asked whether on a previous occasion he had given information to police about others involved in crimes, Scott at first denied this but after more questioning admitted the salient point to be true. He had thought that such matters were strictly between the police and himself, but now it was out in the open he offered an apology to the judge and jury. Not surprisingly, defence counsel asked the jury to disregard this evidence, giving his opinion that it was a "sad reflection on the Crown's case that Scott had been called as a witness".

There was nothing much left to come of the Crown's case, save scientific testimony. Forensic scientist John Bark, who had examined the car left at Gatwick, confirmed that he had found blood inside and out. A smear of blood on the front of the saloon could have been made by the movement of a hand, while fairly heavy stains on the back, some running down to the number plate, were consistent with a blooded body being heaved into the boot. He was satisfied that there had been no fight inside the vehicle because he had found only small spots of blood there. He concluded that Sergeant had been bleeding heavily from his wounds when his body was placed in the car and that anyone handling the body would have got blood on his clothes.

The scientist Bark went on to describe how he had examined Lloyd's clothing and his silver-coloured Volkswagen Polo car. None of Sergeant's blood had been found on anything belonging to Robert Lloyd.

He had also inspected a shotgun recovered from Lloyd's brother's caravan at Woodlands Farm and declared that there was nothing in forensic terms to link the killing with that gun or with the farm. He had also examined the two shotguns belonging to Lloyd himself and could say with certainty that two of the three wounds on the body could not have been inflicted by either gun.

It was a very satisfied defence counsel who summed up the case on the final day. Far from showing, as the police believed, that Sergeant was shot near Woodlands Farm, all the scientific evidence was to the contrary. Far from aiding the prosecution, the experts had shown with increasing clarity that the odds favoured Lloyd's version. Simpson declared triumphantly: "It makes a nonsense of the theory that the defendant lured Mr Sergeant to Woodlands Farm and shot him, and the idea that he got a gun from the mobile home at the farm without Jimmy knowing, got him somewhere else then shot him, does not bear serious examination."

The jury of seven men and five women took just over an hour to declare Robert Lloyd, now 31, not guilty, and as the verdict was announced there was clapping, cheering and tears of relief from a group of friends and relatives at the back of the court.

Whoever shot Jimmy Sergeant did a very professional job. The vital weapon disappeared from sight. Not a soul could remember seeing the car dumped at the airport, or got sight of its driver. The money vanished. The keys evaporated. The tell-tale clues that so often fall into the hands of forensic scientists, especially when bodies and cars are found, were not found.

Someone, surely, must have known who the killer was. But no-one gave him away, no-one sought the reward. That tempting £50,000 was never claimed.

9

GET THE PRIME MINISTER!
The Brighton Bombing, 1984

No-one gave him a second glance as he stepped out of a taxi on the Brighton seafront, quickly paid the driver and strolled through the revolving doors of the Grand Hotel. Neatly groomed, smartly dressed and unobtrusive, there was nothing to distinguish him from the dozens of other figures moving through one of the resort's busiest and most popular hotels. He might have been there for a sales conference or just to spend a quiet weekend by the sea.

No-one who saw him during the following three days could remember anything significant about his features. Neither his taxi driver nor the hotel receptionist could recall if he had any luggage with him.

It was a typically busy Saturday lunchtime at the hotel. Although the peak of the summer trade had passed, and the managers were preparing for the much busier autumn conference season, many people were coming and going.

The clock showed mid-day as the new arrival asked the receptionist for a room, said that he wanted to stay until Tuesday and – perhaps unusually – stated that he would pay by cash, in advance, in full.

He produced the required £180 from a wallet and scribbled a few pen entries on the hotel registration card:

Date: Saturday, September 15, 1984;

Name: Roy Walsh;

Address: 27, Braxfield Road, London, SE4;
Nationality: English
He left the space for passport number blank and signed his entry, "R.Walsh".
The receptionist offered him room 629. High up on the sixth floor, with magnificent views across the English Channel, the room would have been much in demand in busier periods. R. Walsh accepted the room without question, took possession of the keys and made for the lift. He spent three days and three nights within the sumptuous surroundings of the Grand, and there he met a companion.

R. Walsh was undoubtedly a cover name for one of the IRA's most daring bomb planters. His companion almost certainly one of their most important bomb makers. Their mission was to carry out the most daring act of terrorism since Guy Fawkes.

Although the intelligence services must have had their theories, a name was never put to the second man; he did not book into the Grand but presumably took lodgings nearby, where he could more safely store the parts of a lethal device. By calling at the hotel simply as an unchecked visitor he was able to smuggle in the pieces he required, bit by bit.

There seems no doubt that this "active service" team was in place within an hour of Walsh's arrival. At 12.55 p.m. Walsh went to the hotel's main restaurant, where his guest joined him for a quiet meal followed by one cup of tea and one glass of milk. Some of the other twenty or so lunchers – including the hotel manager, whose table was nearby – noticed them but paid them no particular attention. They charged the meal to room 629. And it would seem that they did not appear in the public restaurant again, preferring to eat in the room.

Several members of the hotel staff spoke to both Walsh and his companion from time to time, but afterwards they had only the sketchiest memories of the two men.

However, there were two significant encounters, both by waiters called to bring food or drinks to 629, which later became extremely important to the police.

The first was on Sunday, September 16, when the two ordered sandwiches and tea during the afternoon. The waiter distinctly remembered being answered by a male voice when he knocked on the door. A tall man of about 6ft 2ins, who was not Walsh, turned away from him and spoke in the direction of the bathroom door, saying simply "They're here". The waiter assumed that the other man was inside the bathroom, and he assumed that he was Walsh.

Over twenty-four hours later, at 10.00 p.m. on Monday, September 17, the

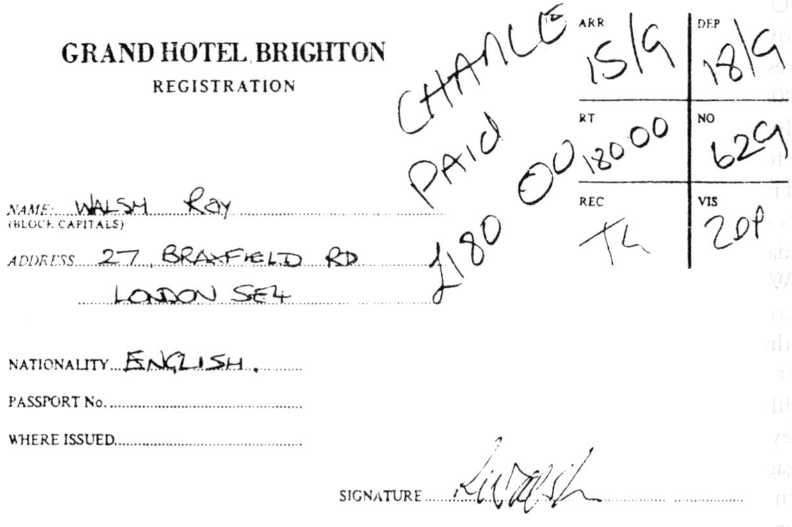
GRAND HOTEL BRIGHTON

REGISTRATION

NAME: WALSH Ray
(BLOCK CAPITALS)

ADDRESS 27 BRAXFIELD RD
LONDON SE4

NATIONALITY ENGLISH.

PASSPORT No.

WHERE ISSUED

SIGNATURE

CHANCE PAID £180 00

ARR 15/9	DEP 18/9
RT 18000	NO 629
REC TL	VIS 20P

Registration card completed by one of the Grand Hotel bombers. A vital piece of evidence in the ensuing investigation.

night porter received a call from 629 requesting a bottle of vodka, three bottles of coke and some glasses.

Sussex police are certain that the two conspirators spent their Sunday and Monday assembling a bomb which they then placed beneath the bath in room 629, concealed behind the detachable front panel.

The bomb parts were relatively small – easy to smuggle into the hotel in a briefcase or small suitcase. There were three essential components to the device: the timer-power unit, about the size of a video cassette; a PP9 battery about 6in high and 2in wide; and the explosive itself, about 25 pounds of gelignite.

Thanks to modern printed-circuit technology, a bomb like this can be set to go off days, weeks, or even months into the future. Walsh and his co-conspirator would be long gone before the explosion. As a final touch, they introduced a delicately balanced anti-handling device, probably a mercury tilt switch, wired to the inside of the bath panel. Had security men gone to the lengths of removing all the hotel's bath panels the chances are they would have set it off.

The "magic" of the device was contained in the integrated circuits of the

TPU, the timer-power unit. The police became convinced that unit placed below the bath at the Grand was from a batch that the IRA had hidden at Salcey Forest in Northamptonshire for use by their active service units who, early in the 1980s, became active on the British mainland.

In the January of 1984 bomb-squad detectives had recovered six TPUs from the forest, part of a larger arms cache. They were housed in plywood containers and neatly numbered from 1 to 7 – except that number 4 was missing. Laboratory tests established that they were each set to go off after a precise time delay – of 24 days, 6 hours and 32 minutes. They were all accurate to within one minute.

When the full story of the Brighton bomb emerged, the implications of this discovery became starkly significant – TPU number 4 had been removed for use by the Brighton based team.

It has been calculated that Walsh and his companion had completed their highly dangerous task at 8.21 p.m. on the evening of Monday, September 17. They would have waited for at least one more hour for the printed circuits to engage automatically after completing the manual settings. Once 9.21 p.m. had been reached they could expect to be home and dry, safe in the knowledge that their part in the venture was done, the bomb primed and set.

The vodka and cokes ordered from the night porter at 10.00 p.m. may well have been for celebratory drinks, although alcohol is also a very effective solvent, so it is just possible that these meticulous operators washed their hands in the spirit and toasted one another in the soft drink.

They say that the best IRA active service units are so confident in their handiwork that they will sleep alongside their bombs. Walsh certainly did spend that Monday night sleeping in room 629, though the chances are that his friend simply slipped away into the night to begin packing for home.

The last that was seen of Walsh was on the Tuesday, when, between 9.00 a.m. and 10.00 a.m., he handed in his room keys, settled his meal account of £56.50 and booked out.

Several guests used room 629 during the following three weeks and relaxed in hot baths only inches above the device. But the police had no reason at that time to make a thorough search of the bathrooms, nor did they consider it essential during the run up to the Conservative Party's annual conference, set to begin in the second week of October.

The Tories were in a jubilant mood that year having overcome the dark days of the 1982 Falklands war and gained a landslide victory at the General Election of June, 1983; as the party faithfuls came flooding into Brighton for the annual ritual of mutual admiration they could not be blamed for some degree of self-satisfaction, knowing that the Government was sitting on a 144-seat majority, the biggest since Labour's 1945 victory, and still with more than three years of office to run.

Terrorism was certainly an issue of the times. The IRA had been attacking London targets – they killed Tory MP Airey Neave in the House of Commons car park in 1979, caused devastation in Hyde Park and Regents Park in 1982 and bombed Harrods just before Christmas 1983. But there was nothing to indicate that they had Brighton in their sights. The security measures taken by Sussex police before the Conference were fairly stringent, but it seems fair to say that they were designed more with the prospect of general public disorder in mind, than with any question of an assassination attempt.

Security at the Grand Hotel became very strict in the week beginning October 8. Mrs Thatcher already had her personal protection unit in constant attention and her accommodation in the first-floor Napoleon Suite, just refurbished in a £500,000 hotel facelift, was banned to all but her closest associates, the entrances well guarded.

Indeed, the first floor became a mini-fortress to which entry was prohibited except for those in the highest security category. It was thoroughly searched by men and sniffer dogs. Electronic listening systems were in place and a 24-hour watch was kept on monitors from which a cluster of surveillance cameras was controlled.

In the rest of the hotel, uniformed and plain-clothes policemen patrolled each floor under the command of an internal control centre. At the front entrance, officers monitored the arrival of all visitors, and carried out checks on individuals and their baggage.

At the nearby Brighton Centre, where the set-piece conference sessions were taking place, precautions were even more strict – security men checked the bags of all visitors, no-one could get in or out without proper authorisation and a large part of the frontage was cordoned off from passers-by.

Certainly Grand Hotel manager Paul Boswell, supervising his 21st political conference, was of the opinion that security was tighter than he had ever known it.

Later there were to be criticisms of the exercise – that baggage checks were not thorough enough; that rooms were not searched carefully enough; and that too big a concentration of police resources went into a blanket wall of protection on the first floor, leaving the other floors comparatively neglected.

It was also questioned whether it was advisable to accommodate so many of the country's leading politicians together in the same building. Practically every member of the government had been neatly stacked in a batch of rooms one above each other, like so many ducks in a fairground shooting gallery. That was something not likely to happen again after Brighton.

But, of course, it was easy for the critics to have their say in hindsight. With the revolutionary long-delay timer in position five storeys above the crucial first floor, with the gelignite packed tightly out of the range of passing sniffer dogs, the men from room 629 already held the initiative, and they must have followed – at a comfortable distance – the gathering array of political stars with a growing sense of wonderment.

The IRA had been extremely lucky. Walsh had not chosen his room, it had been allocated to him at random, and there is no evidence to suggest that he had any prior knowledge of where the Tory guests would be staying in the hotel. Yet by stroke of fortune, the bomb was resting on the sixth floor directly above the room occupied by Margaret Thatcher and her husband Denis. They were in room 129. Room 128 was occupied by the foreign secretary, Sir Geoffrey Howe. In rooms dotted around them were nearly all the other significant men of the Tory government – industry secretary Norman Tebbitt, chief whip John Wakeham, chancellor Nigel Lawson, environment secretary Patrick Jenkin, party chairman John Gummer, home secretary Leon Brittan, agriculture minister Michael Jopling, education minister Sir Keith Joseph and health minister Norman Fowler.

While they did not choose their room, the IRA team surely knew exactly what they were doing when they set the automatic timer. It was primed to go off in the middle of the night, when they could be reasonably certain that most of the conference guests would be in bed. And it would go off just hours before Mrs Thatcher was due to deliver her keynote speech which, by tradition, brings the closing Friday session to a crescendo of cheers and a standing ovation.

One of the security cameras placed at strategic points around the hotel looked down on the fine Victorian facade and the array of bedroom windows that faced out to sea. It was focused on the first floor. This camera automatically recorded on videotape the precise moment the bomb went off. It recorded the time – 2.54 a.m. Friday October 12, 1984, and a billowing cloud of smoke and dust erupting from the sixth floor and cascading downwards into the levels below.

As the dust settled, the spectacular scene was revealed. An ugly gash had been rent down the front of the building, with debris spewing across the main A259

The scene at the Grand Hotel shortly after the explosion. *(Photo: Evening Argus)*

Norman Tebbit is rescued from the rubble. *(Photo: Evening Argus)*

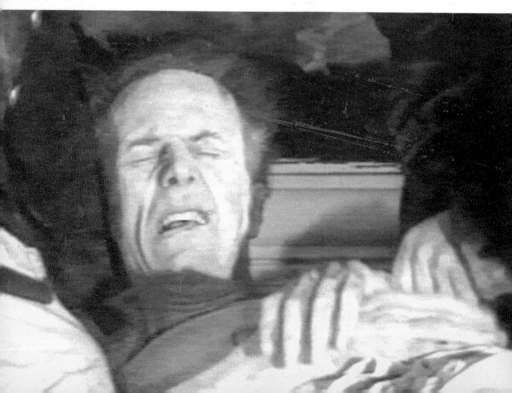

Firemen, harnessed to more secure parts of the building, continue their search of the shattered building by daylight. *(Photo: Evening Argus)*

road and hundreds of yards outwards on to the promenade and beach. Inside, six complete rooms on six successive levels had collapsed downwards like a tumbling pack of cards in a horrific jumble of masonry, timber, furniture and personal possessions which cascaded deep into the basement kitchens. The grotesque pile of mangled wreckage filled the basement and towered up like a mountain through what was once the ground-floor foyer and up into the first floor.

Seconds after the rooms were reduced to rubble, a massive chimney came toppling down to add to the mountain; a 15,000-gallon water tank in the roof was split asunder, dousing everything below; live power cables were left sparking; timbers and girders were left poised at crazy angles; where there once stood magnificent bedrooms, now there was a black chasm.

Inside the mass of indistinguishable debris were nine human beings, some dead, some struggling for life.

Those who survived will never forget the first minutes afterwards – the non-stop ringing of alarm bells, the cascading water, the feeling of helplessness, the fear of what more there might be to come, the panic that rescue might not arrive in time.

The brunt of the huge explosion was borne by a group of four rooms, numbers 628 and 629 on the sixth floor and 528 and 529 immediately below on the fifth.

Closest of all to the 25 pounds of explosive was 52-year-old Mrs Jeanne Shattock, wife of the Western Counties Tory Association chairman Gordon Shattock. There seems little doubt that at the time of the explosion she was in the bathroom of Room 628, which was divided only by a thin wall from the bathroom of 629. The force of the explosion hurled her through the collapsing walls, across a corridor and into the wreckage of the room next door, number 638, where she was instantly covered by rubble. More than twenty-four hours passed before firemen found her mutilated and decapitated body, with fragments of ceramic bathroom tiles embedded in it like shrapnel.

While his wife died instantly, Gordon Shattock had a truly miraculous escape. One moment he was comfortably dozing, the next he was sparked into full consciousness by the blast and a terrifying flash behind the bathroom door. In a matter of seconds he was flung from his bed and began falling down what must have seemed an endless pit. Aware of concrete pieces descending alongside him, he held himself in a tight ball as he floated down on fast-moving debris past floors five, four, three, two and one, through the foyer and deep into the basement. To his astonishment he found himself alive and able to walk. He made his own way out of the building, virtually unscathed. One of the first people to talk to him was a Brighton fireman, who asked, "Where did you come from?" to which Mr Shattock replied, "Express lift from the sixth floor!"

All five rooms below 628 collapsed into a gigantic heap of debris. Three people in them died, five were saved.

The chairman of the North West Conservative Association, 54-year-old Eric Taylor fell from the fifth floor into the ground-floor foyer area, where he was smothered by heavy debris. For a time rescuers were able to talk to him. "My name is Eric", one heard him call. He died there and it was not until midnight on the next night that they were able to retrieve his body. His wife, who had been sharing 528 with him, fell into the basement but, like Gordon Shattock, picked herself up and walked away.

Government chief whip John Wakeham, resident on the fourth floor, fell as far as the foyer, where rescuers later pulled him out with multiple injuries. His

45 year-old wife Roberta had died alongside him.

Close by them at foyer level were the MP for Enfield Southgate, 59-year-old Sir Anthony Berry, and his wife Sarah, who had fallen from the third floor. Sir Anthony died, while Lady Berry survived thanks to beams that supported the massive weight of rubble above her leaving her just enough space to breathe.

A hospital doctor called to the scene, Dr David Bellamy, spotted two hands poking out from the rubble. One belonged to Norman Tebbitt and the other to his wife, Margaret. He was able to squeeze them and offer comforting words that rescue was on the way.

Norman and Margaret Tebbitt fell the shortest distance, from room 228 on the second floor, but they were trapped high up in the tower of debris. He was trapped in a foetal position, with cuts and broken bones. Only feet away from him, his wife had back injuries and was to be paralysed from the neck down.

Earlier in the week Norman Tebbitt had called the National Health Service "the linchpin" of the country's health provision. He was rescued after a four-hour ordeal and whisked off to the Royal Sussex County Hospital for an unexpected taste of NHS treatment. Thousands of television viewers saw him carried from the wreckage.

There were many strokes of good fortune. On the first floor, room 128 vanished from sight, but its occupant, Sir Geoffrey Howe, had decided to stay on at a late-night conference party and was not even in the hotel. He had missed the event completely.

Conference organizer Harvey Thomas plunged down two floors from room 729 to 529, and was buried in rubble. He survived, but with rib injuries. He remembered calling out "Help" as rescuers arrived. They kept him in conversation as they tried pinpoint his position. "Don't worry I'm not going anywhere", he responded. In fact, he was precariously poised on the edge of the chasm left by the vanished floors, pinioned by a pile of rubble that might have fallen at any moment. During a delicate 90-minute operation a group of firemen pulled him out.

The secretary of the Conservative Foreign and Commonwealth Council, 72-year-old Mrs Mabel de la Mott, was hurled from her bed in room 529 into a corridor. She had multiple cuts and bruises, but after digging herself out of rubble she found her own way to safety down a fire escape.

Margaret Thatcher had been putting final touches to her Friday speech in room 129 on the first floor and at around 2.45 a.m. was about to use the bathroom before joining her husband Denis in bed. But she was interrupted by her private secretary, Robin Butler, who came into the room and handed her a set of papers. As she was checking through them the bomb went off six floors above.

The prime minister's escape was a close-run thing. The impact of the blast caused the collapse of rooms 628, 528, 428, 328, 228 and 128, only yards from where she worked. A slightly different positioning of the device might have easily demolished 629, 529, 429, 329, 229 and 129, leaving her and Denis Thatcher under tons of rubble.

Masonry from the toppling flight of rooms came crashing through Mrs Thatcher's bathroom ceiling, leaving it a wreck. It was only by chance that she was not in the bathroom at the time. The bedroom remained intact and the prime minister, her husband and her staff were able to congregate in an office until firemen arrived and led them from the hotel to the safety of Brighton police station.

Astonishingly, room 629, where the bomb had been planted, was only partially destroyed, the main force of the blast having powered through the bathroom wall into 628. The occupants of 629 were Scottish Tory Party chairman Donald McLean and his wife Muriel, who were buried where they slept under debris from the room above. Mr McLean survived. His wife had her right leg amputated below the knee in the Royal Sussex County Hospital and later died in the intensive-care unit there.

The final tally was a grim one – five dead, thirty-two injured, some seriously. But the IRA had missed what must have been their prime targets, the prime minister and her senior cabinet ministers.

When, nine hours after the explosion, the Provisional IRA in Dublin put out a statement to the Press Association, they claimed to have detonated a 100-pound gelignite bomb "against the British Cabinet and the Tory warmongers". The statement continued:

Thatcher will now realise that Britain cannot occupy our country, torture our prisoners and shoot our people in their own streets and get away with it. Today we were unlucky, but remember, we have only to be lucky once; you will have to be lucky always. Give Ireland peace and there will be no war.

While the nation was still coming to terms with the shock, and with recriminations mounting over what was seen to be lax security, the Sussex police and Scotland Yard began the task of catching the killers. Before the dust had settled, and certainly before some of the bodies had been recovered, the serious detective work was under way, led by Detective Chief Superintendent Jack

Reece, head of Sussex CID, Detective Superintendent Bernie Wells, head of Brighton CID, and Commander Bill Hucklesby, head of Scotland Yard's anti-terrorist squad. They were to call on a team of 112 Sussex police officers and another 30 from the anti-terrorist unit during the enquiry, using a fully computerised incident room at Brighton police station, a satellite incident room at the Yard and supported very extensively by the Interpol network.

Despite early fears that a second device might be in place, and the risk of the building collapsing on them, detectives began foraging through the debris in the search for clues. The "scene of crime" search covered the wrecked building, the littered road outside and the stony beach.

Unusual objects, clothes, limbs were all important while even the shoes of people leaving the scene were brushed in case they had picked up minute components.

The nature of the device was at the time not known, so the possibility that it had been planted that night had to be considered. A team of policemen went straight to the hospital to interview injured victims. There were many others to speak to as well, some shocked and dazed, still in their night wear. Many were moved to the Metropole Hotel next door, which itself had to be evacuated for a short period during a second bomb scare there.

Inevitably there were numerous false trails, some disposed of quickly but others occupying much police time. Witnesses told of a group of Irishmen who had been making jibes about the Tories in the Metropole on the night of the blast. A very credible witness had seen a man of Iranian appearance with Afro hairstyle running from the scene and had given chase. Another "strange man" with blue rucksack had been spotted sitting in the foyer of the Grand at 2.30 a.m., only 15 minutes before the turmoil began.

But the most likely suspect to emerge in those frantic first days was a thinly built man of about 35 with a chest-length beard who had been spotted by a chambermaid entering room 629 just before the conference began. He had a key to the room, and slung over one shoulder was a silver-coloured case, of the kind often used to carry photographic equipment but which could equally well have carried explosives. For a time the police had him top of their wanted list, issuing a detailed artist's impression which occupied many front pages and appeared on ITN. The publicity resulted in 76 calls from the public. Eventually, though, the bearded man with the silver case was said to be an "innocent repair man with legitimate business" on the sixth floor. What that "legitimate business" was no-one said. Maybe the man was more of an embarrassment to the police than was admitted – just possibly, he was an electronics expert employed by the security services to plant listening devices.

The enquiry was on a larger scale than anything ever before experienced in Sussex. Officers collected 4,000 dustbins full of materials from the scene and sent them to the Yard's forensic laboratory at Woolwich. They traced every Grand Hotel resident on the night of the bomb and spoke with them. Then they set out on the daunting task of tracing all staff who had been employed at the Grand during the previous three months, and all residents who had used the vital rooms 528, 529, 628 and 629 between August and October.

This was an immensely difficult and complex assignment. Guests had come from all over the world, including America and Africa, and some were away for illicit weekends their close families did not know about. Discretion was needed. No fewer than 800 enquiries were made through Interpol in fifty different countries, the biggest single enquiry ever undertaken by them, before the job was completed. But, in the end, the police traced and eliminated all the guests who had stayed in the four rooms over the past three months.

That is, all except one – Mr Roy Walsh of 27, Braxfield Road, London, SE4.

The address was genuine and police officers spent much time talking to the occupants of number 27, who had lived there for 30 years. They questioned neighbours, residents in nearby roads, and called on pubs and clubs in the area. The name Roy Walsh was given out on the BBC Crimewatch programme, was published in the national press and was passed to police stations throughout Britain and other law-enforcement agencies throughout the globe. Families with the name Walsh were visited, included some who lived in Northern Ireland.

But no-one could be found who knew a Roy Walsh who had been to Brighton for a recent holiday, or who had stayed at the Grand, and as the weeks passed the police became more and more convinced that he was the man they sought.

His hotel registration card, the most significant clue to emerge after the hundreds of interviews and the thousands of man hours that had occupied the inquiry over many weeks, became Exhibit Number One.

Key members of the hotel staff were fingerprinted and the prints compared to those found on the card. Some matched of course, and they were eliminated. But one set of prints could not be identified and it was on these that one of Scotland Yard's most experienced fingerprint experts, David Tadd, was asked to concentrate his equipment and skills. Using laser techniques and a chemical called ninhydrin, which reacts to the amino-acid content in sweat, he was able

The Thatchers' bathroom in their suite at the Grand Hotel showing how close the bombers came to achieving their target.
(Photo: Evening Argus)

to reveal a right palm print on the front of the card to the left of the signature line as well as the print of a left little finger nearby.

A Yard team then began comparing the prints with those on their file of known major criminals and, particularly, with those of known terrorists with Irish connections.

Almost exactly three months after the bombing, on January 17, 1985, Jack Reece and Bernie Wells of the Sussex police were called to the Yard for a highly confidential briefing by Commander Hucklesby and his senior aides. The Yard men revealed that the prints on the hotel card matched those of Patrick Joseph Magee, a 35-year-old Belfast man who was well known to the police as a member of the IRA and currently active in terrorism on the mainland of Britain and in Europe. His popular nickname was "Chancer".

There was already a substantial file on Magee. He was wanted by the anti-terrorist squad in connection with the London bombings of 1979. He had been arrested in Holland in 1982, but an application for his extradition to this country had sensationally failed. Thanks to that the British authorities had lost sight of him.

The police kept this fingerprint identification a close secret. Obviously if Patrick Magee were to learn that he had become The Most Wanted Man in Britain he would go to ground, disappearing either into the safety of the Republic or to some friendly location abroad.

Bernie Wells admits that it was hard to have to tell people that no progress was being made, while the small team of detectives was in fact elated by the result of the forensic work and now firmly believed that success was very close.

The only hint that anything had changed came when Scotland Yard re-issued a set of wanted posters of well-known terrorists. Placed unobtrusively in the middle was a photograph of Patrick Magee.

It is unlikely that the events of the following five months will be revealed for many years to come, so sensitive and secret were they. The British intelligence services must have been instructed to put all their resources into finding Magee. Under-cover operations must have stretched throughout the whole of Ireland, in the North and in the Republic, much of Britain and parts of the continent, wherever the trail led. How many men risked their lives to get close to IRA sources we do not know. What lengths they went to is not clear. But the result was a remarkable success for the security services, perhaps their biggest-ever victory over Irish terrorism.

In the early summer of 1985 a new IRA active service team of young men and women gathered in Scotland to plan a spectacular series of explosions in London and seaside towns across the nation. They planned to plant 16 bombs, with timer-power units set for either 24-day or 48-day delays, in 16 different locations to explode on consecutive weekdays between July 19 and August 5. Four of the bombs were intended for London, the others for the resorts of Brighton, Bournemouth, Eastbourne, Dover, Folkestone, Ramsgate, Blackpool, Great Yarmouth, Torquay, Margate, Southend and Southampton.

The terrorist group had split into two squads, known as Team A and Team B. By early June, Team A had already planted one device in London, on a 48-day timer which was set to explode late in July. Team B was preparing to plant their devices, with 24-day timers, at a number of seaside resorts. One of them had committed their programme to paper. It was: Brighton (June 25), Torquay (June 11), Bournemouth (July 3), Southampton (June 17), Blackpool (June 29) and Eastbourne (July 1).

Had the plot succeeded, it would have meant bombs going off on successive days at the height of the holiday season, across the length and breadth of England. It would have cost many lives and many injuries. It might even have engendered a panic. Certainly it would have given the IRA its biggest success ever.

It was prevented in the nick of time by the men seeking the Brighton bombers. In the middle of June the security men had pinpointed Magee's likely whereabouts to a particular road and a particular flat in Glasgow. Strathclyde police, led by Detective Chief Superintendent Ian Robinson assembled a team of twenty-three officers, eleven of whom were trained marksmen issued with firearms, to carry out a surprise raid on Saturday, June 22, 1985.

They swiftly cordoned off Langside Road in the city suburbs and while the bulk of the men surrounded a block of flats, a small front-line group of armed officers knocked on the door of a two-bedroomed ground-floor flat that had been rented nine days previously by a man and a woman. Patrick Magee answered the door. He was immediately recognized by Detective Sergeant Dennis Innes who, acting with great initiative, grabbed him and passed him back into the hands of colleagues waiting behind.

As the officers entered the hallway four more people emerged from the kitchen, where they had been having a meal. Innes, aided by Detective Inspector Ian Forsyth grabbed one man, manhandled him into the living room and removed a loaded 9mm Browning automatic pistol from the waist of his trousers. Later, they learned that this was 34-year-old Gerald McDonnel, an escapee from the Maze Prison in Northern Ireland in 1983. The other three – Peter Sherry, aged 30, Martina Anderson, 23, and Ella O'Dwyer, 26 – surrendered quietly, overwhelmed as they were by numbers of armed men. All five were arrested under the Prevention of Terrorism Act and taken into custody.

Inside a money belt that McDonnel had been wearing the police discovered something rarely found in operations against the IRA – actual documentary evidence of proposed crimes. It was the programme for the holiday bombing campaign. The Strathclyde police had not only found Magee, they had un-covered a plot more threatening than the Brighton bombing itself.

The "code" of the programme was soon cracked. From it the police worked out the proposed time-table for the sixteen carefully planned explosions. The first nine were due to have 24-day timers, the last seven 48-day. If the letters BT appeared, it meant that device was booby trapped. MTS meant that a mercury tilt switch was fitted. If a line was ticked, it meant that the timer had already been set. In some columns the letters "H" and "B" appeared. These police assumed meant either hotel or beach, depending on which location would prove most suitable.

During the search of a cellar at James Gray Street, close to Langside Road, the police discovered sufficient explosive and bomb-making materials for the assembly of fifteen devices, along with a range of timer-power units each marked with intended locations and dates. Some of the timers were already set and running. They had no doubt that all the items belong to the five.

Most chillingly of all, they realized from these remarkable finds that one bomb had already been placed. Fortunately, details in the calender of death gave them enough information to do something about it. The relevant column read: "Monday, July 29, 1985. Time 1300t. Location London. First floor, 112, Ruebens Hotel, Buckingham Palace Road. BT plus 48."

Bomb-disposal men arrived there during Sunday, June 23, and inside Room 112 they found the device, hidden in the well of a bedside cabinet. Explosives and a 48-day TPU were found packed inside a plastic lunch-box together with a mercury tilt switch that would have set the bomb off had any resident or employee touched it. The expert who defused the bomb confirmed that it would have exploded at 1.00 p.m. on July 29.

The anti-terrorist squad became convinced that it had been planted by Magee only a couple of weeks before, when he had stayed for one night at the Reubens hotel, giving a false name and address.

Magee and his companions were flown from Glasgow to London two days later and at Paddington Green police station on June 27 the two Sussex policemen Reece and Wells confronted the man they had pursued for so long. They put to him various questions about the Brighton bombing, but Magee never said a word. He spent the whole session staring down at the table between them.

All five suspects were charged with unlawfully and maliciously conspiring together with other persons unknown to cause explosions likely to endanger life or cause serious injury to property in the United Kingdom. Magee alone faced seven further more serious charges, which included planting the Brighton bomb, causing it to explode, and murdering the five victims who had died in the aftermath.

The police made no secret of the fact that others were obviously involved, both at Brighton and in the foiled seaside terror campaign. But they had not been traced.

There was unprecedented security at the Old Bailey in London in May 1986 when the long trial began. Sniffer dogs searched the court, roads were closed, police marksmen lined rooftops and a helicopter hovered over the convoy of police vehicles that brought the accused in. For the first time, everyone entering the court had to pass through an electronic security gate. Outside, a small group

Mrs Thatcher – a remarkable escape. *(Photo: W. Sussex County Times)*

of demonstrators stood waving banners and chanting their support for the five.

The three men and two women denied all the allegations against them and listened placidly as prosecutor Roy Amlot described the plot "to create havoc and bloodshed throughout the country". The Brighton attack was "one of the worst acts of terrorism ever in Britain" and had "come within an inch of being the Provisional IRA's most devastating explosion", he said.

The 25-day hearing revealed for the first time the full story of the bomb that nearly killed a British prime minister. It also revealed the stunning reality of a seaside terror campaign that might so easily have changed the summer of 1985 into a bloodbath. But perhaps the biggest sensation was reserved for the defence lawyers to produce: they claimed that the police had framed Magee.

During his closing speech on the 19th day, defence counsel Richard Ferguson alleged that police had "selected" his client Patrick Magee to be "the villain of the piece."

Mr Ferguson stressed that it was an allegation that he did not make lightly, but he believed that when detectives had learned that Magee had no alibi for September 15-18 they had planted his fingerprints on the registration card at the Grand Hotel.

The Yard already had a set of his prints at the time of the bomb and all they had to do was to "transfer" them to the card, alleged the lawyer. It had taken experts many weeks between the October and the January to establish the identity of those prints. But if Magee's prints had been left genuinely on the card, they could have been checked out and confirmed in a matter of days. He went on:

> You can imagine the furore which followed this bomb. Whose fault was it, why didn't someone anticipate, what about the security, how did someone get so close to wiping out the Prime Minister and her Cabinet?

> You may think the only way the police could redeem themselves was to find someone as a defendant and to charge him or her with the Brighton bombing.

> There was no other way they could retrieve their credibility. That, we say, is what happened and Magee was the likely suspect....

It is true that it took the police more than two months to isolate the vital Magee fingerprint on the registration card, but is that time delay so surprising? It was weeks before they could eliminate all the many guests who had stayed at the Grand between August and October and the registration card of Roy Walsh did not become suspect until it was realized that no trace of its owner could be found. Only then was it subjected to specialized analysis.

Sergeant Innes was accused by defence counsel Martin Thomas Q.C. of planting the Browning automatic pistol on McDonnel during the Glasgow arrest, something he strongly denied. Another defence lawyer, Stephen Solley, claimed that Sherry had been at the Glasgow flat only "by a complete fluke" and now stood accused of being a bomb plotter through association with the others.

But the jury was not convinced. All five were found guilty.

After the verdict the judge, Mr Justice Boreham, addressed Magee:

> You have been convicted of eight dreadful offences – seven of them that horrifying bombing of the Grand Hotel at Brighton. Five people murdered in their beds, others seriously injured, some of them still completely disabled and others who had escapes which were nothing short of miraculous.

> You intended to wipe out a large part of the Government and you very nearly did. If that was not enough, within a few months you were plotting an even more hideous campaign – much more cynical, completely inhuman, not caring about political or military targets but aimed at ordinary men, women and their children on holiday in the height of the holiday season.

> This is the most cowardly enterprise which it has ever been my misfortune

to listen to. These are crimes of an exceptional gravity. You are a man of exceptional cruelty and inhumanity. You enjoy your terrorist activities. You plan them meticulously and with affection.

Members of the public must be given the maximum protection I can provide.

When brought into the dock for sentence, Magee refused to answer to his name and it was left to Mr Justice Boreham to say: "That is the man who was convicted as Patrick Joseph Magee." When he refused to stand, two prison officers were obliged to bring him to his feet. Watching him from the public gallery was his wife Eileen, who wore a T-shirt decorated with a Gaelic slogan *Tiocfaidh Ar La*; in translation, "Our Day Will Come". These same words were repeated by McDonnel as he stood smiling in the dock, arms folded across his chest, as friends called back at him from the gallery.

All five defendants received life sentences, Magee eight times over.

Just one month after the conclusion of the trial a £10-million restoration of the Grand Hotel was completed and the now even more splendid 162-room hotel was re-opened – with a new security team and a brand-new computerized room-locking system.

Two years later, in the October of 1988, the Conservatives returned to Brighton and the Grand for their Autumn conference, exactly four years after the bomb ordeal. Margaret Thatcher said then:

Four years have passed since we last came to Brighton for our conference. We all have memories of that week, memories sad and memories brave. But the human spirit is indomitable. We will not bargain, not compromise, nor bend the knee to terrorism.

The only note of irony was the massive security operation that accompanied her return. All police leave was cancelled. Some 270 tons of reinforced concrete blocks were moved on to the seafront and 400 metal barriers erected as Sussex Police created an "exclusion zone" around the hotel and conference centre. Armed officers were on alert 24 hours a day. A police helicopter dominated the sky above. The Navy was on alert in the Channel. A 24-hour computer system automatically checked the comings and goings of all conference goers through new personal security cards. Pillar boxes were sealed. Police divers searched drains under the Grand. Even the SAS was said to be lurking in the shadows. In all, the exercise cost £1.4 million, the biggest single security operation ever mounted in a British town.

Adams, George 26
Amlot, Roy 157
Anderson, Martina 155
Albright, Betty 35, 46
Appleton, Sgt. 81
Ashby, Dr. Michael 100, 104
Ashby, Nicole 50
Askew, DS Ambrose 28, 30/1
Avory, Mr. Justice 14
Bark, John 139
Barrett, Supt. Tom 82
Beard, John 12
Bennett, Sir Henry Curtis 14
Berry, Sir Anthony 149
Berry, Lady Sarah 149
Birkett, Norman 44/5
Blok, Anthony 134
Bodkin Adams, Dr. John 86-105
Boreham, Mr. Justice 158/9
Boswell, Paul 144
Box Copse 51/2, 55, 58, 60
Bradnum, Julia 97, 99
Brighton magistrates 44
Bristow, Sgt. 52
Brittan, Leon 145
Bronte, Dr. Robert 31/2
Brown, Judge 119
Budgen, Supt. Isaac 26
Burlin, Arnold 76, 82
Calcutt, Thomas 124
Cameron, Donald 24
Cameron, Elsie 20-33
Camps, Dr. Francis 98, 99
Cassels, J.D. 15, 17, 31
Challen, Robert 57, 58, 61
Cheal, Det. Supt. Douglas 127, 131/2
Clements, Frank 57, 58, 61
Cocks, David 134
Cohen, Sefton 14
Coldicott, Elizabeth 22, 28
Coman Doyle, Sir Arthur 32
Cosham, Florence 22
Crowborough 22/3, 27/8
Crumbles 8, 19
Darling, Mr. Justice 6
Dean, Det. Insp. 57
Devlin, Lord Justice 100, 104/5
Donaldson, Ch. Insp. 36, 38, 42/8
Dorchester Assizes 6
Douthwaite, Dr. Arthur 100, 102, 104
Duke of Norfolk 51, 56, 108, 116
Duncan, Ethel 8-10, 14, 17
Duran-Deacon, Olive 77-8, 80/4
Edwards, Insp. George 26, 30
England, Cecil Louis 34, 40
Ferguson, Richard 157
Fowler, Norman 145
Gillan, Ch. Insp. John 28, 30/1
Goodsell, PC Thomas 30
Gourd, PC 42
Groombridge station 23, 26
Guildford Assizes 6
Gummer, John 145
Haigh, John George 65-85

Hailsham Magistrates 13-14
Hamer, Betty 67
Hannam, Det. Supt. Herbert 94, 98
Harman, Dr. John 104
Hart, Alan 46
Harris, Dr. 92, 94
Harrison, Det. Chief. Insp. Gordon 112/5
Henderson, Archie 72-76, 82
Henderson, Rose 72-76
Heslin, Det. Sgt. Pat 81, 82
Hollis, Dan 116, 119, 121/2
Hoskins, Percy 100
Hewitt, Det. Sgt. 96
Howe, Sir Geoffrey 145, 149
Hucklesby, Comm. Bill 151, 153
Hullett, Gertrude 92-100, 104
Hullett, Jack 92, 97, 104
Humphreys, Judge Travers 85
Jacks, Thomas 60
Jackson, V.H.O. 61-62
James, M.V. 101
Jenkin, Patrick 145
Johnstone, Ch. Supt. Charles 115
Jones, Edward 72, 79, 81
Jopling, Michael 145
Joseph, Sir Keith 145
Kaye, Emily 5-19
Kaye, Violet 34
Kennedy, Michael 118-120
Knight, Stephen 46
Lambourne, WPS Maude 80
Lane, Constance 80
Lawrence, Geoffrey 100-102, 104
Lawson, Nigel 145
Lewes Assizes 14, 44, 84, 105
Lewis, Jane 107-108
Lewis, Jonathan 108/9, 112/3, 116, 122
Lloyd, Michelle 128, 132/3, 136-38
Lloyd, Robert 128, 132-34, 136, 139
Lloyd, Thomas 133
Lustgarten, Edgar 32
Lynch, Dr. Roche 45
Mahon, Ch. Det. Insp. Guy 83
Mahon, Mavourneen 5, 11, 19
Mahon, Patrick 5-19
Magee, Patrick 153-59
Mancini, Tony 34-48
Manningham-Buller, Sir Reginald 100-104
Maxwell Fyfe, David 84
Mayo C.W. 13
Metcalfe, Amanda 118, 122
McDonnel, Gerald 155, 158-59
McLean, Donald and Muriel 150
McSwan, Amy 68, 71, 82
McSwan, Donald 68, 71, 82
McSwan, William 68, 70, 82
Morgan-Harris, James 116
Morrell, Edith 90, 91, 96-99, 104
Moysey, Ethel 39
Narborough, Det. Ch. Insp. Fred 53/7, 61, 63
Neave, Airey 144
Neil-Miller, Clara 97, 99
Normanton, Helena 32
Notyre, Jack 34, 42

O'Dwyer, Ella 155
Officer's House, Langney 8, 13, 19
Pattison, Det. Sgt. 53, 57
Petley, Nelly 61
Philpott, PC John 30
Piper, Agnes 22, 23
Price, Mrs. Annie 28
Pugh, Det. Insp. 96
Reece, Det. Ch. Supt. Jack 150, 153, 156
Roberts, Edward 50
Rundle, Simon 128, 132, 136
Sands, Albert 26
Savage, DCI Percy 12/3
Scott, Gary 138
Sergeant, James 125-139
Sergeant, Arthur and John 131
Shattock, Gordon and Jeanne 148
Shawcross, Sir Hartley 84
Shera, Dr. Arthur 94
Sheriff, Ida 50, 55, 59
Sherry, Peter 155, 158
Silverman, Leslie 119
Simpson, Robin 134, 138
Simpson, Dr. Keith 52/3, 83, 99
Skylark Cafe 35, 42
Sommerville, Dr. 94
Spooner, Det. Supt. Reg 61, 63
Sorrell, Sgt. 36
Spilsbury, Sir Bernard 9/17, 30/1, 36/7, 43
Stephens, Barbara 69
Stevenson, Melford 99, 101
Stillwell, Thomas 52, 56/7, 60-62, 64
Stronach, Nurse 100-102
Surrey Assizes 68
Symes, Det. Ch. Insp. Shelley 80, 82/3
Tadd, David 152
Taylor, Eric 148
Taylor, Supt. William 109, 111/2
Tebbitt, Margaret 149
Tebbitt, Norman 145, 149
Thatcher, Denis 145, 150
Thatcher, Margaret 124, 145, 149, 159
Thomas, Harvey 149
Thorne, Norman 20-33
Triplow PC 42
Wakeham, John 145, 148
Wakeham, Roberta 149
Wallace, Colin 106-124
Wallace, Eileen 108, 122
Walsh, Roy 140-43, 145, 152
Waring, Eddie 106, 119
Waterloo 10/1/2
Webb, Det. Insp. Albert 80, 82
Wells, Det. Sup. Bernie 151, 153, 156
Wesley Poultry Farm 22-24, 28
West, Dr. Iain 112, 115
Whitton, Matilda 89
Wilson, R.P. 60
Wood, Det. Insp. David 133/4, 137/8
Woodhouse, Joan 49
Woodhouse, Thomas 50
Worthing station 51, 54
Yellowlees, Dr. Henry 84

160